Upgrading the EU's Role as Global Actor

Institutions, Law and the Restructuring of European Diplomacy

Michael Emerson
Rosa Balfour
Tim Corthaut
Jan Wouters
Piotr Maciej Kaczyński
Thomas Renard

Centre for European Policy Studies (CEPS)
Egmont - The Royal Institute for International Relations
European Policy Centre (EPC)
Leuven Centre for Global Governance Studies,
University of Leuven

The Centre for European Policy Studies (CEPS) is an independent policy research institute in Brussels. Its mission is to produce sound policy research leading to constructive solutions to the challenges facing Europe. The views expressed are entirely those of the authors and should not be attributed to any institution with which they are associated.

ISBN 978-94-6138-052-4

© Copyright 2011, Centre for European Policy Studies and the authors.

All rights reserved. No part of this publication may be reproduced, stored in a retrieval system or transmitted in any form or by any means – electronic, mechanical, photocopying, recording or otherwise – without the prior permission of the Centre for European Policy Studies.

Centre for European Policy Studies
Place du Congrès 1, B-1000 Brussels
Tel: (32.2) 229.39.11 Fax: (32.2) 219.41.51
E-mail: info@ceps.eu

TABLE OF CONTENTS

PREFACE i
1. Summary and Conclusions 1
   1.1 Purpose 1
   1.2 Analytical and legal framework 3
   1.3 Upgrading the EU in international relations 6
   1.4 The costs of non-Europe ... and the restructuring of European diplomacy 10
   1.5 The new diplomacy 12
2. Why should the EU be strongly represented in the international arena? 14
3. Legal Basis in the Lisbon Treaty and International Law 21
4. Hybrid Combinations of the EU & Member States in International Relations 37
   4.1 Categories 37
   4.2 Guidelines for representation of the EU and member states 39
   4.3 Overview of the status quo and looking ahead 40
5. Restructuring of European Diplomatic Services 47
   5.1 Setting up the European External Action Service (EEAS) 47
   5.2 The costs of non-Europe and the restructuring of European diplomacy 52
6. Status Quo & Perspectives for Selected International Organisations, Conventions, Agreements & Summitry 65
       6.1.1 UN General Assembly 65
       6.1.2 UN Security Council 68
       6.1.3 International Monetary Fund 70
       6.1.4 World Bank 75
       6.1.5 Food and Agriculture Organization (FAO), IFAD and WFP 76
       6.1.6 International Labour Organization (ILO) 77
       6.1.7 UNCTAD 78
       6.1.8 UN Development Programme (UNDP) 78

- 6.1.9 Development cooperation 78
- 6.1.10 UN Environment Programme (UNEP) 80
- 6.1.11 UN Framework Convention on Climate Change (UNFCCC) & Kyoto Protocol 82
- 6.1.12 World Health Organization (WHO) 84
- 6.1.13 World Trade Organization (WTO) and World Customs Organization (WCO) 85
- 6.1.14 International Maritime Organization (IMO) and related agreements 86
- 6.1.15 Bank for International Settlements (BIS) and financial market regulation 88
- 6.1.16 Other economic organisations and regulatory agencies 90
- 6.1.17 International courts 91
- 6.1.18 UNHCR (refugees), Human Rights Council, IOM (migration) 93
- 6.1.19 Arms control – conventions and organisations 94

6.2 European and Euro-Atlantic multilateral organisations 96
- 6.2.1 OECD and IEA 96
- 6.2.2 Council of Europe, European Convention (and Court) for Human Rights 98
- 6.2.3 OSCE 99
- 6.2.4 European Economic Area (EEA) 101
- 6.2.5 EBRD 101
- 6.2.6 Energy Charter Treaty 102
- 6.2.7 Energy Community Treaty (for South-East Europe) 102
- 6.2.8 NATO 102

6.3 Semi-institutionalised summitry and diplomacy 105
- 6.3.1 G7/8/20 105
- 6.3.2 Bilateral summits (strategic partnership cases) 108
- 6.3.3 European neighbourhood and other multilateral regional processes 108
- 6.3.4 Conflict prevention/resolution 112

Glossary 115

Annexes 117
    Annex A. Overview of EU Participation in the UN System....................117
    Annex B. International Organisations and Conventions in which the EU Participates fully by virtue of a Regional Economic Integration Organisation (REIO) or Regional Integration Organisation (RIO) clause 120
    Annex C. Overview of EU Participation in International Maritime Organizations 123
    Annex D. Voting Weights on the Board of the IMF 125
    Annex E. Voting Weights on the Board of the World Bank, before and after 2010 Reform 126
    Annex F. Constituencies on the Boards of the IMF and World Bank 127
    Annex G. Shareholdings in the EBRD (capital subscribed in € mil.) 128
    Annex H. Constituencies on the Board of the EBRD.................................130
    Annex I. Extracts from the Lisbon Treaty 131
    Annex J. The Common Visa Application Centre in Moldova..................135
    Annex K. Statement by the E3+3 with the support of the EU High Representative following the adoption, 9 June 2010, of UN Security Council Resolution 1929 on the Iranian nuclear programme..........136
    Annex L. Draft Resolution A/64/L67 of the UN General Assembly – Participation of the European Union in the work of the UN 137
    Annex M. UN General Assembly Voting on Motion to Adjourn the Debate on Participation of the EU in the UN, 13 September 2010..139
    Annex N. Staffing in the Foreign Services of the EU and the MS 141
    Annex O. Budget Expenditure on Diplomacy of the EU and Member States [a] 142
    Annex P. Aid (ODA) Expenditures of the EU and Member States and Administering Departments 143

List of Boxes

Box 1. Lisbon Treaty – objectives of the EU's external policy
(TEU, Article 21).. 17
Box 2. Lisbon Treaty – legal competences in external affairs 29
Box 3. Treaty texts referring to the EU as a
Regional Economic Integration Organisation (REIO) or Regional
Integration Organisation (RIO). 33
Box 4. G-20 Communiqué of Finance Ministers and Central Bank
Governors on IMF reform, 23 October 2010 [extract] 73
Box 5. European Banking Authority - International relations,
Article 18 89
Box 6. EU coordination and representation in OECD,
in implementation of the Lisbon Treaty 97

List of Tables

Table 1. Competences of the European Union according to the 'Lisbon Treaty', and participation of the EU institutions in related international organisations and conventions....................................... 23
Table 2. Staff and financial resources of European diplomatic services 53
Table 3. Scenarios for restructuring European diplomacy 55
Table 4. Voting weights in the IMF and World Bank, and GDP shares........ 72

List of Figures

Figure 1. Provisional Organigramme of the European
External Action Service (EEAS) 50

Preface

This report has been produced by a group of EU policy analysts based at research institutes in Brussels and Leuven. It was stimulated by the evident challenges of implementing the Lisbon Treaty in the area of external relations. It has been prepared with a view to presenting our findings to the second joint annual conference of Brussels-based think tanks on major European issues, to be held on 25 January 2011.

At the time of writing, the European External Action Service (EEAS) is in the course of being set up. Its formal start date was 1 December 2010, while its effective start date is understood to be 1 January 2011. At the same time there are intricate ongoing negotiations on both the budget and staffing of the EEAS and on the precise forms of external representation of the EU in international organisations and negotiations. Unfortunately, there are continued inter-institutional disagreements over the details here, alongside some signs of back-tracking by member states over an effective implementation of the Lisbon Treaty in the external domain. Further, questions related to the budget and staffing seem likely to become issues in the next multi-annual budget framework after 2013, which will begin to be negotiated in 2011. All this is going to further divert energies from addressing the substantive issues for EU foreign policy. While we regret these continuing arguments and uncertainties, the present contribution provides at least a reference, as an independent view of how the Lisbon Treaty might be implemented and dynamically followed through, and against which actual developments can be monitored.

Contributions by Ludvig Norman, Sven Biscop, Antonio Missiroli, Agnes Sebastyen, Anne van der Lingen, Sergio Carrera, Alejandro Eggenschwiler and Jean Pascal Zanders are gratefully acknowledged.

Thanks also for helpful comments in their personal capacities from Roderick Abbott, Veronique Arnault, Poul Christoffersen, Steven Hodgson, Mercedes Janssen Cases, Lars Lundin, Frederik Naert, David O'Sullivan, John Richardson, Pedro Serrano de Haro, David Spence, and Veronika Wand-Danielsson. None of the foregoing individuals, however, is at all responsible for the views expressed here.

Michael Emerson & Piotr Maciej Kaczyński
Centre for European Policy Studies (CEPS)

Rosa Balfour, European Policy Centre (EPC)

Jan Wouters & Tim Corthaut
Leuven Centre for Global Governance Studies, University of Leuven

Thomas Renard
Egmont - The Royal Institute for International Relations

January 2011

1. SUMMARY AND CONCLUSIONS

> *Abstract*
>
> *This report investigates two crucial factors that will in part determine whether the innovations and ambitions of the Lisbon Treaty for the EU as foreign policy actor will be realised: first, the status of the EU in the multitude of multilateral organisations and international agreements that deal with matters of EU competence, and, secondly, the structure of European diplomacy (i.e. the personnel strengths and costs of the 27 member state diplomacies alongside the new European External Action Service). The report has an original information content since so far there has been no systematic account available on either of these subjects. Going beyond this information function, the report also formulates recommendations for where the EU's status in the international arena is inadequate; and forward-looking scenarios for the restructuring of European diplomacy, which is a task for the next decade or two. Our premise is that the EU should seek to build up a world-class diplomatic corps, capable of becoming a major actor in global affairs. There are interest groups in national foreign ministries that prefer to stick to the status quo, and seek to minimise the restructuring of European diplomacy. However, in our view as independent analysts, fundamental changes in the nature of global affairs mean that this conservatism is indefensible, and would only result in an increasingly obsolete, irrelevant and wasteful European diplomacy.*

1.1 Purpose

The subject of this report, the institutional place of the EU in the international system, now becomes an urgent and inescapable part of the strategic challenge that Europe faces in the world. The status quo is not conducive to the EU's interests. Without revision of the roles of the EU and its member states in the international system, they together will cease to be the multilateral order's best friend, but instead could become an obstacle to its reform and modernisation.

Are we overdramatising the situation? We think not; the writing is on the wall. At the December 2009 Copenhagen climate change summit, the multiplicity of vocal European leaders saw themselves all sidelined at the top table. In September 2010, the EU's attempt to get enhanced participation rights at the UN General Assembly was set back (perhaps only temporarily) by the lack of support mainly from developing countries. In October 2010 the EU member states yielded to the combined pressure of the US and the BRICs (Brazil, Russia, India and China) to cede seats and votes in the International Monetary Fund (IMF), failing which they likely would have been blamed for blocking reform.

Of course everybody is aware that the world outside the EU is changing dramatically, with the huge shift in global power towards Asia and the BRICs, while the processes of globalisation reveal alarming systemic failures at the global policy level, such as in financial markets and climate change policy. The rise of the BRICs also poses questions about the nature of the normative principles (if any) in the newly emerging world 'constellation', and whether the new multi-polarity will degenerate into new balance of power games leading to instability, or worse, conflict.

The EU says in its official documents and countless speeches that it wants to work towards a more structured global multilateral order as a prime objective of its foreign policy. But for this it needs to engage in the upgrading, rationalisation and concentration of its external representation in a radical and comprehensive manner. When the weak effectiveness of EU foreign policy is raised in conversation with national diplomats, we hear bland remarks that there is no appetite for change in the status quo. On the contrary their top priority often seems to be a rearguard action to minimise the innovations of the Lisbon Treaty.

These postures are seemingly oblivious to two twin dramas: first, the need for the EU to get organised to face the new global challenges, and second, the budgetary case for restructuring European diplomacy in the light of acute macroeconomic needs to reduce wasteful expenditure at all levels.

Actually, the entry into force of the Lisbon Treaty, with the creation of the post of High Representative/Vice-President of the Commission (HR) and the European External Action Service (EEAS) and granting of legal personality to the EU as a whole, make for a golden opportunity to review the existing arrangements for the representation of the EU in the international system. This concerns the whole complex landscape: multilateral organisations, international agreements and the less formal but highly important summit diplomacy.

The present report addresses the question of how the EU could rationalise and strengthen its collective diplomacy. It deals only with institutional arrangements, leaving aside the ultimately more important matters of substantive foreign and security policy. Institutions are of course not everything, but they still provide the necessary framework for action. The EU is well accustomed to debates between institutionalists and pragmatists. Both have their arguments, but this report sticks to its purpose, which is essentially the institutional question.

1.2 Analytical and legal framework

The insertion of the EU into the international system is already rather impressive, and a good basis for further improvements. Over the last few decades, the European Community – now the European Union (or EU) as its legal successor – forged a relationship with a great number of multilateral organisations and became a party, usually with the member states, to a huge number of international agreements: 249 multilateral treaties and 649 bilateral treaties are recorded in the European Commission's data base of treaties. However this mass of relationships has developed in a dispersed and *ad hoc* manner, leaving problems of inconsistency and obsolescence with regard to the institutional and policy development of the EU.

The EU has inherited from the European Community a variety of different types of status in multilateral organisations and treaty schemes:

o the EU as member or contracting party,
o the EU as 'virtual' member or 'enhanced' observer (i.e. full functional participant, except without vote or full formal status) and
o the EU as 'ordinary' observer.

At the same time the EU's member states are generally full members, or contracting parties, and through the Council also have the role of mandate controller for the EU's participation where this is significant.

The Treaty on the Functioning of the European Union (TFEU) for its part sets out several categories of EU competences:

o exclusive competences,

- shared competences, of which there are several types, including 'parallel competences', the 'coordination' of economic policies, etc. and
- policies where the EU may undertake actions supplementary to the member states.

In principle there should as a matter of institutional logic be consistency between these sets of categories. The practice is not totally devoid of logic, but should be more clearly ordered, and in many cases an upgrade of the EU's status in the international sphere where the TFEU confers competence appears justified by the level of its competences. To devise operational guidelines for this is however a complex task, since it involves three distinct but overlapping categories of issues:

1. *Questions of the status of the EU in existing international organisations*, and in particular whether its present status (as member, or observer, etc.) is in line with actual EU competences as they have developed over recent years in domains such as the internal market (which almost invariably has external aspects), common policies (e.g. transport), economic and monetary union, and common foreign and security policy.

The Lisbon Treaty has clarified and in some cases upgraded EU competences, but is largely silent on these external institutional questions, no doubt because these are not for the EU alone to decide, and on many details the EU must act in close cooperation with its member states and is also dependent on the willingness of third states to upgrade its international actor status. As a first approximation one may envisage the following guidelines:

- In cases of exclusive competences, the EU would be the preeminent actor, subject to mandate-controlling activity by the member states, which might also (but not necessarily) be members.
- In cases of shared competences, the norm would be a hybrid regime with the EU as well as the member states as full members, or with the EU as 'virtual' member where the organisation is engaged more in dialogue and coordination rather than legally binding matters.
- In cases where the EU has some but only weak competences, it would be an ordinary observer.

Where the EU has achieved full status in agreements or agencies of the UN system, it has relied for legal basis in the agreements or statutes of the organisations concerned on recognition of a category called the Regional Economic Integration Organisation (REIO), or Regional Integration Organisation (RIO), to which relevant competences have been delegated. The EU has on these grounds been admitted to the FAO, the Codex Alimentarius Commission and 70 other agreements as full member or contracting party. However, the insertion of such REIO or RIO clause is not a prerogative of the EU and has to be agreed with the contracting parties or member states. In several cases there has been insufficient support for proposals to pass (examples are given below).

2. *Questions of who represents the EU in international organisations, negotiations and fora*, for which the Lisbon Treaty is more explicit, but not without leaving some unsettled questions which need to be sorted out without delay.

The Lisbon Treaty gives clear responsibility to the HR to represent the EU in foreign and security policy (TEU, 27.2), and to the Commission for other domains of EU competence with the exception of the monetary union (TEU 17.1), and also an elaborate procedure for the Council to decide which of them should lead the negotiations, or be head of the negotiating team (TFEU 218.3). The EU Delegations are now in principle well placed institutionally to represent the EU in the main centres of multilateral diplomacy (New York, Geneva, Vienna, etc.) precisely because of their capacity to represent the entire EU – and not just the Commission, as in the pre-Lisbon era – in international organisations, although there are still in some cases frictions over bringing in the new system. There also remain uncertainties over how the interests of member states should be represented in the case of shared competence, especially the so-called 'parallel competences'. These uncertainties should best be ended quickly through an inter-institutional understanding (as appears now to be happening over the 'mercury' case, discussed in detail in section 6.1.10), and if not, by rulings of the Court of Justice, to settle institutional and procedural questions which still occupy all too much time at the expense of substantive issues.

3. *Questions of reform of the multilateral system,* which have become a matter of increasing urgency and importance with the rise of new powers which claim a corresponding increase in their presences in major international organisations, and which leads to consequent pressures for the so-called 'advanced' countries – meaning mainly Europe – to make room for them. This underrepresentation of new

powers also coincides with the underrepresentation of the EU itself (a new power of a different kind), and so connects with the sensitive issue internal to the EU on the relative position of the member states and the EU itself in these organisations.

Overall the status quo in relation to all three questions is far from satisfactory. In many instances – especially regarding shared competences – the EU's status lagged behind the development of the EU's competences even before the Lisbon Treaty, and now all the more so with the Treaty's innovations in the foreign and security policy and the area of freedom, security and justice. There are unresolved tensions between the EU institutions and member states over who represents the EU in negotiations in certain types of situations. While the pressures for reform in the multilateral system mount, the EU and member states have difficulty in forming consistent positions for the EU to advance while the member states have to give ground. The general strategy may be thought of as shepherding the role of the EU in a considerable number of cases incrementally to a step up in the multilateral organisations, taking into account the realities of EU competences. But everything cannot be done at once. Some selected cases are urgent, while others are clearly only conceivable politically in the longer run. We now summarise a number of important cases.

1.3 Upgrading the EU in international relations

The UN General Assembly (UNGA) has seen the law of unintended consequences at work, with the Lisbon Treaty interacting with the rules of procedure of the UNGA to downgrade the EU's presence. This is because the HR and President of the European Council are tasked with representing the EU in UNGA debates, rather than the member states representing the rotating Council Presidency, and since the EU is not a member of the UN but only one of many 'ordinary' observers, it can only intervene after the 192 UN member states have had their say. This led the EU to propose in September 2010 a Resolution, invoking its status as a RIO, for upgrading its participation to that of 'enhanced' observer at the Assembly and its subsidiary working groups and UN conferences. This proposal suffered a setback when a majority voted to defer rather than immediately pass the Resolution, and this will have to be overcome as soon as possible with the aid of much more thorough diplomatic lobbying by the EU and its member states.

Paradoxically, current arrangements provided in the Lisbon Treaty for the representation of EU positions in the UN Security Council (UNSC) are today more satisfactory, since a combination of EU and UNSC procedures make it possible for the HR to intervene on behalf of the EU where it has a common position to express. The HR began to make such presentations in 2010. At the same time debate over structural reform of the membership of the UNSC, which has been ongoing for decades without resolution, has become intense again with pressures for increased representation of new powers. This debate is highly sensitive for France and the UK as existing permanent members, Germany as a would-be permanent member, and others who would like a still wider membership, in addition to which there is the logical long-run question of the status there of the EU itself. The future of this debate is hard to predict given the number of contradictory positions inside and outside the EU.

Elsewhere in the UN system of agencies and programmes there are a number of instances where the reality of EU competences in relation to the activities in question, including financial contributions, could justify full member status as a REIO or RIO. Examples of organisations where upgrade of the EU to full member is overdue include the ICAO in civil aviation, the IMO in maritime affairs, the ILO in labour market and social policy and the WIPO for intellectual property.

The WTO and FAO provide examples of how the EU and member states can work together when both are members of organisations. The FAO case is especially pertinent with other cases in mind, since this organisation deals with a wide range of issues which for the EU are a mix of exclusive, shared and national competences. But even here there is room for more efficient and cost-effective coordination between the EU and the member states, reducing the number of meetings at which all member states observe negotiations conducted by the Commission on mandates decided in Brussels; in some such instances there could be a thinning out of expensive overrepresentation by member states' diplomats especially at the WTO, and where a single EU notetaker could suffice.

In several UN programmes and conferences (UNDP, UNCTAD, OHCHR, UNHRC), the EU is a mere observer, despite being an important financial contributor and having major policy interests. Lack of full member status leads also to exclusion from Executive Boards or Steering Groups, where the most important policy shaping may take place. At the UN climate change convention (UNFCCC), the EU has full status alongside the member states, but the multiplicity of voices at summit level (especially at Copenhagen in December 2009) has been widely criticised for its consequent loss of effectiveness.

Three European or Euro-Atlantic organisations (Council of Europe, OECD and OSCE) are given special mention in the Lisbon Treaty (Article 220 TFEU), which calls for the EU to develop 'all appropriate forms of cooperation' without saying what these should consist of.[1] In all three cases the EU is only observer. The case of the Council of Europe (CoE) is even more special, since the Lisbon Treaty provides for the EU to accede to the European Convention of Human Rights (ECHR), and negotiations are under way for this. If one accepts the premise that the EU should in principle enter fully into the governance structures of organisations that entail legally binding obligations for EU policies, an upgrading of the EU's status at the CoE becomes a matter for consideration. For the OECD the nature of its business is more dialogue and debate, with fewer legally binding commitments. In this case the current status as 'enhanced observer' may suffice, although a case could be made – especially in light of the composition of the G-20 – in favour of full EU membership. The OSCE is still a different matter: although it is the custodian of fundamental principles and values, such as those laid down in the Helsinki Final Act, the organisation is essentially political in nature and not legal. Moreover, the operationality of the OSCE suffers from its 56 member state composition, which makes its working sessions resemble a mini-UN without the UNSC. The OSCE needs reform to become more effective, for example to create a steering group to facilitate more rapid decision-making. Failing this, there could be less formal initiatives bypassing the OSCE, such as the Medvedev-Merkel proposal for an EU-Russia security dialogue between the HR and the Russian foreign minister, which could be made into a trialogue with the US.

At the IMF and World Bank there are the triple problems of overrepresentation of the member states, non-representation of the EU itself and political obsolescence of the constituency systems of the Executive Boards. The situation reached a crisis point at the IMF in September 2010, where the US implicitly allied with the BRICs to pressure

---

[1] The UN and its specialised agencies are also covered by this article in the same way.

the member states into reducing their over-representation, and EU member states agreed to certain concessions at the G20 finance ministers meeting in Korea in October. Since monetary policy is an exclusive competence of the EU for those member states that have the euro as their currency, the logical solution would be for the eurozone member states to agree to share a common seat and constituency of the Executive Board. The IMF agreement foresees a limited revision of quotas and seats on the Executive Board to become operational in 2012, and for further review eight years later in 2020. Assuming the eurozone recovers from its present crisis, 2020 would be a suitable date to switch to a single seat for the monetary union. In the case of the World Bank, the EU should at least have a seat as observer, and preferably enhanced observer, on the Executive Board.

The G7/8/20 are acting effectively as steering groups for international economic policies. Here the EU is adequately represented through the Presidents of the Commission and of the European Council, or excessively so, with two places in addition to the presence of the larger member states. At some stage it should be possible for the EU to be represented by just one President.

The EU and NATO have extensive cooperative arrangements, but their operationality is limited. Mutual observer status at the level of the North Atlantic Council (NAC) and Political and Security Committee (PSC) would be a possible short-run development, given the official desire to develop an EU-NATO 'strategic partnership' and (in the words of President Van Rompuy) to "break down the walls between our two organisations".

Given the importance of the EU's shared competences which spill over into international affairs it is inevitable that the EU's diplomacy is going to retain a hybrid character indefinitely, even with this substantial restructuring. A federal regime, with the EU to gain exclusive competence for most external relations, is not on the horizon. Instead, the essence of the hybrid system (motor) is to have two sources of power, with the EU and its member states working together. However hybrid engineering is complex, and the EU and member states have to work constantly at eliminating unnecessary procedural complications and expensive duplicative presences at many international fora.

1.4 The costs of non-Europe ... and the restructuring of European diplomacy[2]

The EEAS is now formally established. This involves a merger of relevant parts of the Council Secretariat and Commission in a new body, and the upgrading of the 136 former Commission Delegations into EU Delegations, which are now responsible for all EU competences – political, economic, foreign and security. The EEAS is initially endowed with a total staff at home and abroad of 3,720, and with (proposed) budget expenditure of €476 million in 2011.

By comparison, the 27 member states have 3,164 embassies, missions and consulates worldwide, employing 93,912 staff, costing €7,529 million. Whereas the EEAS budget is €1 per capita of the population, for the 27 member states diplomacies the average cost is €15 per capita. The EEAS will have one staff member per 134,677 of the population, whereas the 27 member states average 1 staff member per 5,335 of the population.

These figures suggest huge scope for economies of scale if the EEAS is able to take on functions that in some cases are currently duplicated 27 times. There are possibilities for this in arranging common political and economic reporting, in establishing common consular services for issuing at least short-term Schengen visas, and in arranging for mini-diplomatic missions to be co-located with the EU Delegations to save in infrastructural costs. In addition there are many international meetings where the EU does not have to be represented by 27+1 delegations (for example technical meetings at the WTO, as remarked above).

But there are more fundamental reasons justifying a radical restructuring of European diplomacy. The very nature of national and European interests has been changing. Apart from simple commercial competition within the EU and between member states, the weight of 'pure' national interests of individual member states in foreign affairs that are different to those of other member states, or which can be advanced without winning support at the EU level, has surely been declining as a function of the twin dynamics of European integration and globalisation.

---

[2] The statistics presented in this section should only be regarded as rough indications. Every effort has been made to extract from comparable data in correspondence with national MFAs and Permanent Representations in Brussels, but there are doubtless cases where this is not completely assured.

At the global level there is an ongoing radical transformation of the very nature of international diplomacy, with the rise of horizontal networking activity with policy shaping by horizontal alliances of official parties and non-state interest groups, alongside limited achievements (and some manifest failures) of top-down summitry. The EU is a leading practitioner of this horizontal networking activity at home, and can aspire to developing these capabilities at the international level, but this has to be based on building up EU-level diplomatic capabilities in many technically complex fields, which cannot be done extensively also at member state level without hugely costly duplication.

We therefore present four scenarios for restructuring European diplomacy:[3]

1. *Minimalist budget-neutrality*. This imposes a zero growth constraint of the budget of the EEAS, and amounts to denial of the purpose of the Lisbon Treaty to build up the role of the EU as global foreign policy actor. It has to be included in our scenarios since it is the closest to what the member states currently appear to be trying to do.

2. *Common sense budget-neutrality*. Involves the transfer of around 380 national diplomats to augment the EEAS in the period 2011 to 2013, without being replaced at home.

3. *Moderate restructuring – with some net budget savings*. The EEAS staff would be doubled up to the year 2020 (increased from 3,720 to 7,440), alongside a 10% (or 9,492) reduction in the staff of the member states' diplomacies, yielding a net budget savings of €283 million for EU and member states' budgets together, i.e. a sizeable amount compared to the initial budget of the EEAS. About one-third of the 3,720 posts are for administrative grade diplomats, which makes about 120 extra posts per year over 10 years (note that the 2011 budget request is for an extra 100 such posts, so the scenario extends roughly this rate of expansion).

4. *Substantial restructuring – with larger net budget savings*. Under this scenario, the EEAS staff would be tripled (increased by 7,440 to 11,160) but here the time horizon might be until 2030, thus continuing a steady rate of staff expansion, alongside a 25% (or 23,729) reduction

---

[3] Data used in these scenarios on MFA costs are detailed in section 5.2 below and in annexed tables.

of the member states' diplomacies, yielding a net saving of €948 million for the EU and member states' budgets together. This would raise the staff strength of the EEAS roughly to the level of the top three member states' diplomacies.

Various member states are now already making cuts in their foreign ministry budgets in this range of 10 to 25%, and in the cases we can observe (Austria, France, Poland, Slovenia and the UK) these cuts are being implemented over short to medium-term time horizons. This means that net budget savings in the scenarios 3 and 4 would be front-loaded in the next five years, in keeping with current budgetary imperatives. Moreover the countries cited do not include the most acute current budget crisis cases (Greece, Ireland and Portugal), which may be making deeper cuts. But these scenarios deal only with the cost side of a cost-benefit analysis. The benefit side is impossible to quantify but even more important, since this is about transforming European diplomacy's performance into 'punching its real weight'. To contribute to this the 'substantial restructuring' scenario would seem more plausible than the 'moderate restructuring'. Regrettably, there is no sign that the are taking an integrated view of their overall budget and policy priorities (national and EU combined), by profiting from economies of scale in strengthening EU diplomacy alongside a slimming down of wasteful national diplomacy.

1.5 The new diplomacy

Way above the minutiae of arguments over who exactly should represent the EU in various fora is the challenge for the EU as a whole, as for all the world's major powers, to adapt their diplomacy to the new and fast-moving realities of global governance. A leading academic reference from the other side of the Atlantic sees the achievements and potential of the EU in this context more clearly than most Europeans do.[4] This is a world of "disaggregated sovereignty", characterised by "a tightly woven fabric of international agreements, organisations and institutions that shape states'

---

[4] Anne-Marie Slaughter, *A New World Order*, Princeton, NJ: Princeton University Press, 2004. The author has since in 2009 become head of the policy planning staff of the US State Department. In the quoted lines, the author is also citing Abram and Antonia Chayes, *The New Sovereignty: Compliance with International Regulatory Agreements*, Cambridge, MA: Harvard University Press, 1995

relations with each one another and penetrate deeply into their internal economics and politics". In this situation the new sovereignty may be defined as "the capacity to participate in international institutions of all types". The new sovereignty (and new diplomacy) is about status and membership, thus "connection to the rest of the world and the political ability to be an actor within it". The EU is in several respects uniquely well placed to connect with this world of ever-more complex international regulatory structures: it is already contracting party to hundreds of international agreements, it pleads for a stronger international law based on world order, and has worked out institutionally more thoroughly than anyone else out how internally to implement supranational law at the national level. All the internal regulatory departments of the Commission are already engaged in the international dimension of their sectoral policies. The Lisbon Treaty enhances the EU's legal capacity to participate in international institutions of all types. The creation of the new External Action Service, led by a High Representative who is also Vice-President of the Commission, provides the perfect opportunity for the EU to succeed in the new diplomacy combining traditional foreign and security policy matters and the rising mass of global regulatory activity. The new EU Delegations are empowered to represent the EU across this entire landscape. This model for a new European diplomacy requires two further prerequisites to become a reality: a sustained, systematic and well organised push to progressively enhance the EU's status in organisations where this lags behind its actual competences, and the steady build-up of a world-class diplomatic service with competence in both traditional foreign policy matters and extensive sectoral regulatory policies. The present report is devoted to setting out the details of these two prerequisites.

The extent and complexity of the outstanding issues, for short- to longer-term time horizons, warrant a White Paper to be drawn up by the HR and Commission, proposing a comprehensive and strategic approach both for the short-run and the medium-term future through to 2020. The experiences of the second half of 2010, in the UNGA and the IMF in particular, demonstrate the need for a strategic approach, which when adopted will also require the combined diplomacies of the EU and the member states to work for its acceptance by the rest of the world community.

2. WHY SHOULD THE EU BE STRONGLY REPRESENTED IN THE INTERNATIONAL ARENA?

In a nutshell, the response to the question posed above is because the world is changing profoundly, and the EU and its member states have to do so as well in order to remain relevant in world affairs.

The institutional provisions in the Lisbon Treaty to strengthen EU foreign policy (the HR, EEAS, etc.) were overdue. The structures of European diplomacy have become grossly obsolescent, ineffective at the world level and wasteful of precious talent and budgetary resources. The existing structure of European diplomacy is chronically out of line with major structural changes in international affairs that have already occurred and are gathering increasing momentum: globalisation and the rise of new great powers, the changing nature of diplomacy with declining relative weight of bilateral inter-state affairs and the increasing demands to work out mechanisms of global governance. The EU has some chance, if it organises itself properly, to have a significant say in global affairs; the member states acting individually and with different discourses have little or no chance of being effective at the level of strategic significance.

Expression of doubt can be heard these days in the informal talk of some foreign services of the member states whether the provisions of the Lisbon Treaty should be followed through strongly. Some would minimise its effectiveness. But for these 'conservatives' the writing is on the wall. At Copenhagen in December 2009, President Obama went alone to try and negotiate with China, India and Brazil, since there were too many European leaders to take along with him. In Washington in September 2010, the United States forced the EU member states into defensive concessions over their representation on the IMF Executive Board, while the European Central Bank (ECB) has only the limited status of observer. Either the member states agree to follow through Lisbon with a major restructuring of European diplomacy, or they consign themselves (as independent US commentators are saying with brutal clarity) to irrelevance in global affairs, and a very expensive irrelevance at that.

While we turn to matters of administrative organisation of European and national foreign services below (in section 4), some fundamentals are first discussed. The organisation of the new European diplomacy should reflect how the realities of 'national interests' and 'European interests' and their interdependence have been evolving. Several types of 'national interests' can be observed in practice:

1. *Where the member states have 'pure national interests'* that are matters neither of intra-MS competition nor of EU common policy, for example the promotion of Hispanic culture in Latin America, or the extension of Italian citizenship more widely to the Italian diaspora.

2. *Where the member states have interests in competition with each other.* Here ordinary commercial competition evidently remains, although the integration of European corporate structures blurs this, and common concern for the EU's economic competition with other world powers rises in importance.

3. *Where the member states have regional priorities that differ*, but where they are obliged to blend these into the priorities of the EU as a whole in order to pursue them effectively. The North versus South divide is an obvious and major example, but one where the result has been the formulation of common policies for both, since individual member states need the resources of the EU as a whole to back their interests. The attempt by President Sarkozy in 2008 to transform the EU's Mediterranean policy into the preserve of its Mediterranean member states was a spectacular illustration of the failed pursuit of 'national interests' outside the EU framework.

4. *Where the member states have thematic priorities that differ, but where they are compelled to negotiate together common positions*, without which they cannot have effective policies. Here the major example is over the weights to be given to political values versus commercial or security interests. Experience reveals cases of cracks in common positions, for example where some member states are seen to be keener than others to shift a common EU position away from political priorities in favour of commercial interests.

Such differences in national preferences may be visible, but the member states are still compelled to resolve them, failing which no one gets good results in the long run.

5. *A further category is where the member states may have different propensities or political wills to engage in the use of military force.* Iraq was a case in point, and leaves its imprint on attitudes now in the UK and others who joined the US, versus those who did not. The choice to go to war or not may remain a basic prerogative of the member states, yet this major example of divergent choices over whether to go to war is hardly viewed by anyone as having been a rewarding experience.

6. *Where the member states simply find themselves united with common interests,* thus seeing the merging of the national with the common European interest.

The crucial justification for restructuring European diplomacy is the changing relative weights of these categories. While 'pure' national interests (i.e. those that have no interconnection with common EU interests or processes) still exist, they have a declining share in the foreign policy agenda. There is now a substantial category where divergent national preferences have to be negotiated into the big package of common EU initiatives. Competing commercial interests continue to exist, but pale by comparison with the external competition for the EU as a whole, while European integration and globalisation both work to shape up of common interests. Against these inexorable trends the current predominance of national foreign services of the member states lags behind realities.

Another approach is to review the several interpretations of how the global system (order or disorder) is actually evolving, and how the EU's interests and potential as a global actor may relate to these. We highlight four such interpretations.[5]

1. At the level of high principles, the EU places itself in the *liberal institutionalist school of international relations*. The Lisbon Treaty provides the official view at length, with a long list of normative objectives, without using the word "power" once (see Box 1).

---

[5] For an extensive exposition, see David Held and Anthony McGrew (eds), *Governing Globalisation – Power, Authority and Global Governance*, Cambridge: Polity Press, 2002.

Box 1. Lisbon Treaty – Objectives of the EU's external policy

1. The Union's action on the international scene shall be guided by the principles that have inspired its own creation, development and enlargement, and which it seeks to advance in the wider world: democracy, the rule of law, the universality and indivisibility of human rights and fundamental freedoms, respect for human dignity, the principles of equality and solidarity, and respect for the principles of the United Nations Charter and international law.

The Union shall seek to develop relations and build partnerships with third countries, and international, regional or global organisations which share the principles referred to in the first subparagraph. It shall promote multilateral solutions to common problems, in particular in the framework of the United Nations.

2. The Union shall define and pursue common policies and actions, and shall work for a high degree of cooperation in all fields of international relations, in order to:

(a) safeguard its values, fundamental interests, security, independence and integrity;

(b) consolidate and support democracy, the rule of law, human rights and the principles of international law;

(c) preserve peace, prevent conflicts and strengthen international security, in accordance with the purposes and principles of the United Nations Charter, with the principles of the Helsinki Final Act and with the aims of the Charter of Paris, including those relating to external borders;

(d) foster the sustainable economic, social and environmental development of developing countries, with the primary aim of eradicating poverty;

(e) encourage the integration of all countries into the world economy, including through the progressive abolition of restrictions on international trade;

(f) help develop international measures to preserve and improve the quality of the environment and the sustainable management of global natural resources, in order to ensure sustainable development;

(g) assist populations, countries and regions confronting natural or man-made disasters; and

(h) promote an international system based on stronger multilateral cooperation and good global governance.

Source: Article 21, TEU.

International cooperation or governance is both rational as well as ethically preferable to systems that lead to conflict. This means taming great powers with international norms and multilateral processes, and going beyond the primacy of interstate relations towards the domestication of international affairs. The EU and its member states have come to understand this, and have become leading practitioners both in their own regional integration and in global affairs through supporting the advance of international law. However, to be able to promote this worldview effectively, the EU has to be fully represented and participating in the relevant fora. The message is all the more powerful where there is consistency in the discourses of the EU and its member states, avoiding the twin hazards of cacophony or boring repetition.[6]

2.   A simpler approach is that of *functionalism*, well known to students of European integration, but applying equally to international relations. Functionalist theory is about those functions that national governments are not, or no longer, equipped to handle, and which require structured international cooperation to assure the efficient supply of global public goods. At the practical level this fits well with the plethora of regulatory mechanisms (for products, financial markets, environmental standards) that have to be applied at the global level for effectiveness, and where the EU has a key role in developing such standards and implementing them in its member states. This has led to a dense two-way traffic in regulatory business between the EU and international standard-setting bodies; the EU serving as the transmission mechanism for ensuring effective implementation of global standards at the level of member state; in other cases providing the model for international standards. These processes require that the EU be fully represented at the level of the international bodies or agreements in question.

3.   Opposing these views is the *realist school*, which is all about power and its necessity in order to defend `national` security and political and economic independence. Moderate realists recognise the useful role of various international organisations such as the World Bank, IMF, WTO and

---

[6] As Pascal Lamy remarked at last year's Brussels Forum, 28 March 2010: "It does not make sense if one European takes the floor on one topic, and then another European takes the floor on the same topic. Nobody listens, because either it is the same and gets boring, or it is not the same and would not influence the result at the end of the day. That's how groups work".

UN Security Council, and from an American perspective these were usefully fashioned according to its design and interests as post-war global hegemon. While President Obama seems to favour strengthening multilateralism, the new rising powers all seem strongly driven by realist urges. The BRICs grouping is all about their securing greater power in the world, either formally through bigger voting weights in the international financial institutions (IFIs) or more generally through asserting a higher profile in international affairs. The EU's closest neighbour among the global powers, Russia, vaunts explicitly the rebuilding of its great power status. The EU may want to work towards a liberal institutionalised multilateralism, but with American ambivalence and the rise of the BRICs it faces an uphill struggle. For this the EU has to be powerful in its own way, with a full status and effective organisation of its diplomacy at EU and member states levels in the major international organisations and processes.

4. *Cosmopolitanism* is the last and most recent paradigm that we need to discuss. It shares with liberal institutionalism the need for an extensive set of multilateral institutions and bodies of international law to govern the globalising world.[7] However it is a less state-centric concept, and distinct in emphasising the increasing role of non-state actors and transnational networks, involving both civil society and corporate interests, which work towards the definition of international rules and standards. It recognises the diverse sources of rule-making, political authority and power, with a complex patchwork of overlapping jurisdictions and diverse forms of public-private partnership. The cosmopolitan brand of international relations plays strongly into the potential comparative advantages of the EU as external actor, where the domestic and international are overlapping categories, and where EU and international rule-making activity are integrated with each other.

This short review of paradigms leads to several conclusions. Contemporary globalising trends see a blur of domestic and international policy matters with the rise of global regulatory policies (as opposed to classic foreign policy). This plays in favour of the EU's potential comparative advantage as an international actor, with important roles for

---

[7] David Held, "Cosmopolitanism: Ideas, Realities and Deficits", in Held and McGrew, op. cit.

both the new institutional appointments in the foreign policy domain (HR and President of the European Council), and the Commission in the regulatory fields of its competence. But the overarching concern is that the newly emerging multi-polarity looks ominously dangerous at present for the future of the world, given the weak interest shown so far by the new great powers in building up a normatively founded multilateralism. If the EU's overarching objective is to mitigate these risks with a stronger multilateral order, it has first of all to get itself properly organised for this purpose both in its internal organisation and in its representation in the international system such as it exists. To have any chance of exercising a systemic influence, the EU will have to organise the coherence of its actions across the multiple sectors of foreign policy, from classic foreign affairs to soft security, humanitarian assistance, economic policy, trade, monetary stance, development, etc. This in turn requires strategic coherence in its external representation.

3. LEGAL BASIS IN THE LISBON TREATY AND INTERNATIONAL LAW

The question explored in this chapter is how far the effectiveness of the external representation of the EU might be strengthened in line with, and building upon, the institutional advances of the Lisbon Treaty.

Legal personality of the EU. Article 47 (TEU) confers upon the European Union legal personality, and Article 1 (TEU) says that the EU replaces and succeeds the European Community. Official language communicated by the EU institutions to international organisations with which it has official relations specified the following:

> Therefore the EU will exercise all the rights and assume all the obligations of the European Community, including its status in the Organisation, whilst continuing to exercise existing rights and assume obligations of the EU. In particular the EU will succeed to all agreements concluded and all commitments made by the European Community with your Organisation and to all agreements and commitments adopted within your Organisation and binding upon the European Community.

But do these Articles 1 and 47 do more than maintain the status quo, which is all the above text suggests? Certainly the granting of legal personality to the EU as a whole is enhancing its 'capacity to enter into relations with other states' across the board now for all its competences, including the political, foreign and security domains. While agreements in the latter field were already possible, and actually were concluded, before the entry into force of the Lisbon Treaty, all legal uncertainties in this respect are now removed. The granting of legal personality may therefore be used to strengthen proposals to enhance the status of the EU in various economic and non-economic organisations alike, but has no automatic effect of this kind. This connects with an important category of international actors established in various international agreements, namely 'regional integration organisations', to which we turn below and of which the EU is the prime example.

Competences of the EU. Articles 3-6 (TFEU) lists the EU's competences of several types:

- Article 3, Exclusive EU competences, for trade, competition and monetary policies, and for conservation of marine biological resources;
- Article 4, Competences shared between the EU and member states:
  o First, in 'core' shared competence domains: internal market, energy, cohesion (economic, social and territorial), transport, agriculture, fisheries, freedom-justice-security, environment, consumer protection, and aspects of social and public health (Article 4.2);
  o and with a secondary category of 'parallel competences' for research and development policies where the member states have more substantial competences (Article 4.3-4);
- Article 5, Policies requiring coordination between the EU and the member states, as for economic and employment policies (which are a loose sub-category of the shared competences);
- Article 6, Policies where the EU may engage in actions supplementary to the predominant member states' competences, as for industry, culture, tourism, education, civil protection, and public health; and
- To this list must be added, according to Article 2.4 (TFEU), the shared – or effectively parallel – competence to define and implement a common foreign and security policy, including the progressive framing of a common defence policy, in accordance with the provisions of the Treaty on European Union.

In Table 1 below, this classification is combined with the placing of selected international organisations and agreements within these categories. This should in principle provide some guidance on questions of representation of the EU and member states as between the various models, which we discuss in detail below.

Table 1. Competences of the European Union according to the 'Lisbon Treaty', and participation of the EU institutions in related international organisations and conventions

Competences	Organisations, Conventions	Status of EU & MS
Foreign, security and defense policies (including general political affairs)	UN General Assembly	EU observer; MS members
	UN Security Council	2 permanent MS + 2-3 rotating
	OSCE	EU observer, MS members
	NATO	24 MS
	Non-Proliferation Treaty	MS
	Council of Europe	EU observer, MS members
	G7/8/20	EU participant, some MS
1. Exclusive (Article 3)		
a. Customs union	World Customs Org. (WCO)	Member
b. Competition policy	World Intellectual Property Org. (WIPO)	Observer
c. Monetary policy (for eurozone)	IMF	ECB part observer, MS members
	Bank for International Settlements (BIS)	ECB on Board, some MS
	OECD	EU enhanced observer, MS members
d. Fisheries policy and marine biological	Convention on Fishing and Conservation of the Living Resources of the High Seas	EU & MS members
	UN Conference on Highly Migratory Fish	EU & MS members
	Multiple regional fisheries organisations: Mediterranean, NE Atlantic, NW Atlantic, SE Atlantic, Antarctic, Western and Central Pacific	EU Member & some MS
	Organisations for some species: Tuna, Salmon	EU, no MS

e.	Trade policy	WTO	EU & MS members
		UN Comm.on Internat.Trade Law (UNCITRAL)	EU observer, some MS members
2.	**Shared (Article 4)**		
a.	Internal market	International Standards Organization (ISO)	EU cooperation, MS members
		Codex Alimentarius Commission	EU & MS members
b.	Social policy	International Labour Organization (ILO)	EU observer, MS members
c.	Cohesion (regional)		
d.	Agriculture and Forestry	FAO	EU & MS members
		International Fund for Agricultural Develop.	EU observer, MS members
		Multiple product organisations: Olive oil, Sugar, Cocoa, Coffee, Jute, Tropical Timber, Rubber, Grains, New varieties of plants	EU & some MS members
e.	Environment	UN Environmental Programme	EU observer, some MS members
		UN FCCC (climate change)	EU & MS contracting parties
		Kyoto Protocol	"
		UN Conference on Environmt. and Develop.	"
		Convention on Law of the Sea (UNCLOS)	"
		International Tribunal of the Law of the Sea	"
		International Seabed Authority	
		Protection Marine Environmt. of N. Atlantic	EU & 12 MS members
		Protection of the Danube River	EU & 6 MS members
f.	Consumer protect.	-	-
g.	Transport	International Civil Aviation Organis. (ICAO)	EU observer, MS members
		International Maritime Organisation (IMO)	EU observer, MS members
		Eurocontrol	EU & 21 MS members

h.	Trans-Eur. Networks	-	-
i.	Energy	International Atomic Energy Agency (IAEA)	EU observer, MS members
		International Energy Agency (IEA)	EU participates; 17 MS members
		Energy Charter Treaty	EU and MS members
j.	Freedom, security and justice	International Court of Justice (ICJ)	-
		International Criminal Court (ICC)	EU observer; MS state parties
		European Convention of Human Rights	MS, and in future EU, parties
		UN High Commission for Refugees	EU observer; MS members
		Geneva Convention on Status of Refugees	MS parties, EU plans to accede
		UN Convention Against Illicit Traffic of Drugs	EU & MS contracting parties EU &
		UN Convention Against Transnational Crime	MS contracting parties
k.	Public health, safety	-	-
l.	Research, Technology, Space	International Telecommunicatns. Union (ITU)	EU sector memb.; MS members
		UNCOPUOS (Peaceful Use of Outer Space)	EU observer; MS members
		International Fusion Energy Org. (IETR)	EAEC member, no MS
		Science and Technical Center in Ukraine	EAEC & EU member, no MS
m.	Development and humanitarian aid	World Bank	MS members
		World Food Programme (WFP)	EU & many MS donors
		UNDP	EU observer; MS members
		UNCTAD	EU observer; MS members
3.	**Coordination (Article 5)**		
a.	Economic policies	EBRD	EU & MS members
		OECD	EU enhanced observer; MS members

b.	Employment policies	ILO	EU observer; MS members
c.	Social policies	ILO	EU observer; MS members
4.	**Supplementary (Article 6)**		
a.	Human health	World Health Organization (WHO)	EU observer; MS members
		UN Population Fund (UNFPA)	EU observer; MS members
b.	Industry	UN Industrial Development Org. (UNIDO)	Partnership; most MS members
		Multiple Organisations for commodities: Nickel, Copper, Lead and Zinc	EU & some MS members
c.	Culture	UNESCO	EU observer; MS members
d.	Tourism	UN World Tourism Organization	Most MS members
e.	Education, training, youth, sport	UNESCO	EU observer; MS members
		UNICEF	EU observer; MS members

The procedure to negotiate international agreements. Article 218 (TFEU) establishes the procedure for the negotiation and conclusion of international agreements by the Union. In line with the institutional balance outlined above, Article 218 TFEU refers only to the HR and the Commission, with their respective roles allocated according to matters of CFSP or non-CFSP content respectively.

Precisely because some agreements, mainly framework agreements (association or partnership and cooperation), may cover both CFSP and non-CFSP areas, Article 218.3 establishes a procedure for the Council to take decisions, on the basis of a recommendation by the HR or Commission, "depending on the subject of the agreement envisaged, nominating the Union negotiator, or the head of the Union's negotiating team". The team would be some combination of the HR and of the Commission.

MS are not part of this negotiating team. Nevertheless, if the Council so decides, they may be part of a special committee, with a consultative role ("a special committee in consultation with which the negotiations must be conducted" – Article 218.4). In practice this task is generally given to the pre-existing Council working parties or regional working groups.

The most complex situations arise where the EU and the member states have shared competences, and where the rules are uncertain on how to negotiate on behalf of the member states regarding those areas of shared competences where the Union has not taken action so far.

When preparing the recommendation under Article 218.3, the Commission and/or HR will have to analyse in detail if the areas intended to be covered by the agreement are falling into Union competence, either because they are under exclusive EU competence or because the Union has already adopted legally binding acts in those areas; in case the Union has not (yet) exercised the shared competence at issue, member states are still entitled to adopt certain measures, including at the international level. This must be reflected in a representation of the member states, next to the Union itself. Accordingly, the Commission and/or the HR will have to analyse to which extent the Union has exercised its competence in the shared competence areas intended to be covered by the agreement to be negotiated (taking into account Protocol 25 to the Treaties).

In respect of those issues that fall outside the Union competence, the member states are entitled to negotiate themselves. They may, however, also choose to mandate the Commission and/or HR to negotiate on their behalf, or to mandate some other actor, most likely the rotating Presidency (but other burden-sharing arrangements are possible) to do this. The fact that the Commission and/or HR may be mandated to negotiate on behalf of the member states does not mean that the Union has exercised its competence and taken over the area from member states, within the meaning of Article 2.2 (TFEU). Member states will continue to have the capacity to adopt legally binding acts at national level until the Union adopts legally binding acts in this area. Nevertheless, member states are required by the Treaties to facilitate the achievement of the Union's tasks and refrain from any measure that could jeopardise the attainment of the Union's objectives (Article 4(3) TEU). The 'unicity' of representation in the negotiation may be a key element here.

A different situation arises when the conclusion of an international agreement is necessary to enable the Union to exercise its internal competence, or in so far as its conclusion may affect common rules or alter their scope. In this case, Article 3.2 (TFEU) provides that the Union shall have exclusive competence for the conclusion of such international agreement.

Some cases have recently been under dispute between the Council and the Commission, and may have to be resolved in the Court of Justice, e.g. the UNEP mercury case (discussed in detail in section 6.1.10). The question here was precisely to determine if the conclusion of an international agreement by the Union is necessary for the exercise of its internal competence, or if this may affect common rules, or alter their scope within the meaning of Article 3.2. Somewhat related, there is some discussion as to whether member states can act collectively, but outside the Union, in the areas of shared competences not yet exercised by the Union, or whether such a collective exercise necessarily entails the exercise by the Union of its shared competences.

In order to be more efficient in its external representation, it will be important that there be reached practical arrangements or an inter-institutional understanding to clear up who negotiates international agreements in these cases that concern matters of shared Union competences, but where the member states have still the capacity to adopt legally binding acts (because the Union has not yet exercised its competence). The need for an inter-institutional understanding is high, in particular because in areas of shared competences, and *a fortiori* parallel competences, the exercise by the Union of its competence shall not result in member states being prevented from exercising theirs. In this case, the Union representation will be hybrid, in the sense that the negotiations on behalf of the Union will need to be complemented with negotiations on behalf of the member states. It would obviously be good if there were a clear guide indicating which shared competences are those where the EU has not yet exercised its competence. In practice decisions are taken on a case-by-case basis, typically after complex exchanges in the Council between the legal services of the Commission and the Council over whether the existing legal acts of the Union are such that they largely cover the field or not.

Box 2. Lisbon Treaty – Legal competences in external affairs

Article 1 (TEU). "…The Union shall be founded on the present Treaty and on the Treaty on the Functioning of the European Union …. Those two Treaties shall have the same legal value. The Union shall replace and succeed the European Community."

Article 15.6 (TEU). "… The President of the European Council shall, at his level and in his capacity ensure the external representation of the Union on issues concerning foreign and security policy. Without prejudice to the powers of the High Representative of the Union for Foreign Affairs and Security Policy."

Article 17.1 (TEU). "The Commission shall promote the general interest of the Union and take appropriate initiatives to that end. It shall ensure the application of the Treaties, and of measures adopted by the institutions pursuant to them. …With the exception of the common foreign and security policy, and other cases provided for in the Treaties, it shall ensure the Union's external representation…"

Article 24.1 (TEU). "The Union's competence in matters of common foreign and security policy shall cover all areas of foreign policy and all questions relating to the Union's security, including the progressive framing of a common defence policy that might lead to a common defence."

Article 27.1 (TEU). "The High Representative …, who shall chair the Foreign Affairs Council, shall contribute through his proposals towards the preparation of the common foreign and security policy, and shall ensure implementation of the decisions adopted by the European Council and the Council."

Article 27.2 (TEU). "The High Representative shall represent the Union for matters relating to the common foreign and security policy. He shall conduct political dialogue with third parties on the Union's behalf and shall express the Union's position in international organisations ad at international conferences."

Article 47 (TEU). "The Union shall have legal personality."

> **Article 218.3 (TFEU).** "The Commission, or the High Representative where the agreement envisaged relates exclusively or principally to the common foreign and security policy, shall submit recommendations to the Council which shall adopt a decision, depending on the subject of the agreement envisaged, nominating the Union negotiator or the head of the Union's negotiating team."
>
> **Article 220 (TFEU).** "The Union shall establish all appropriate forms of cooperation with the organs of the United Nations and its specialised agencies, the Council of Europe, the Organisation for Security and Cooperation in Europe and the Organisation for Economic Cooperation and Development. The Union shall also maintain such relations as are appropriate with other international organisations."
>
> "The High Representative ... and the Commission shall be instructed to implement this Article."
>
> **Protocol No 25 (TFEU) – On the exercise of shared competence.** "With reference to Article 2 of the TFEU on shared competence, when the Union has taken action in a certain area, the scope of this exercise of competence only covers those elements governed by the Union act in question and therefore does not cover the whole area."

Who should represent the EU? The question here of who 'represents' the EU is to be distinguished legally and institutionally from the question who 'negotiates' for it (as in the section above), the former involving many dialogue processes which do not result in the conclusion of international agreements. Three possible 'representatives' are identified in the Treaties. The HR is given clear responsibility for representing the EU in all matters that relate exclusively or principally to foreign and security policy (Articles 17.1 and 18.2 TEU). The Commission is given a comprehensive role in ensuring the Union's external representation in all matters except foreign and security policy (Article 17.1 TEU) or when otherwise specified (in particular Article 221 TFEU on the role EU delegations). The new permanent Presidency of the European Council shall represent the EU at his level, i.e. at summit meetings, for matters concerning the CFSP (Article 15.6 TEU).

The rotating Council Presidency is no longer mentioned in the Lisbon Treaty with regard to external relations. From this it might be supposed that the rotating Council Presidency's external representative role is now ended. The Belgian Presidency of the second half of 2010 systematically supported this view, making clear wherever it felt obliged to step in during the transitional period before the EEAS was fully operational that it did so on behalf of the High Representative. However this view is being contested by various member states, first of all by the UK which opposes any moves that might enhance the EU's apparent role as a foreign policy actor, and secondly by the Hungarian and Polish permanent representations in Brussels who are seeking to enhance their forthcoming presidential roles in the first and second halves of 2011 respectively. These arguments are also being played out in a disorderly manner in the several centres of multilateral diplomacy (New York, Geneva, Vienna, Paris), where various ambassadors try to organise alliances in favour of this or that formula for who speaks on behalf of whom, and over details of protocol (nameplates and seating arrangements). The room for argument is provided by the complexity of the EU's legal basis for 'shared competences', as explained in the preceding section on negotiating procedures.

The advocates of a reaffirmed role for the rotating Council Presidency rely on the argument that wherever there are remaining national responsibilities in a field of shared competence, the EU and its member states should together be represented by the rotating Council Presidency. This led recently in the preparations for the December 2010 climate change conference in Cancùn to a situation in which the Council Legal Service had in COREPER to correct assertions of the forthcoming Hungarian Presidency's with the remark that it would be illegal to claim for the rotating Presidency a general role to represent the EU on all matters of shared competence. The waste of energies over these secondary procedural matters is flagrant, and even more serious is the sight of various member states trying to obstruct implementation of obvious intentions of the Treaties with arcane legalisms. The member states are indeed able to designate any one of their number or the Commission to represent them on matters of member states' competence, but it is high time for a sense of proportionality to prevail, and for the member states to be willing to mandate the Commission and the Delegations to represent them as well as the EU itself when there is a manifest need for a demonstrably unified position. Moreover, the fact that the Commission or another EU representative is the spokesperson does not affect the rules on the actual policy-making, which provides for a decisive role for the Council, albeit on proposals of the HR or Commission.

Status of regional organisations in international law. Where the EU (or EC before it) has actually achieved full membership or contracting party status in multilateral organisations or conventions of international law, this has often, especially in the UN system, occurred through acceptance of the category 'Regional Economic Integration Organisations' (REIO) for full status, or virtually full status alongside member states. This has been used in the cases of the WTO, the FAO, various fisheries and maritime organisations and the Kyoto Protocol; and the EU's full membership has also been accepted in other economic organisations outside the UN family such as the Energy Charter Treaty and EBRD. The Commission's Treaties data base in fact records no less than 72 agreements where the EU's full participation is justified by reference to a REIO clause (see Annex B). Objective indicators of regional economic integration can be readily identified, such as custom union, or economic and monetary union. However the texts use only generic language, as for example in the case of the FAO where member states (of the EU) "have transferred competences over a range of matters within the purview of the organisation" (see Box 3).

On the other hand, in the more political foreign and security policy fields, there has been until recently no comparable concept, and the EU has been left as observer even where its competences are of major importance for the organisations concerned, such as in the Council of Europe, OSCE and the UN General Assembly. This is easily explained historically, since the EEC and the EC spent their first decades endowed mainly with economic competences. However with the Lisbon Treaty this situation is now anomalous, with justice and home affairs competences of the EU now firmly embedded legally alongside the former Community competences, with foreign and security policy having become a distinct EU competence, and with the Union as a whole now endowed with single legal personality. However in 2006 there was an innovation in the context of human rights conventions, when the UN Convention for Persons with Disabilities recognised the category of 'Regional Integration Organisations' (RIO), enabling the EU to accede in a manner that better reflects its multifaceted competence well beyond the purely economic sphere. This case uses the same language for the qualifying criterion as for the REIOs, where "member states have transferred competence in matters governed by the present Convention". The most striking anomalies where the RIO principle could be used to justify full EU membership are seen in those cases singled out in the Lisbon Treaty for establishing 'appropriate' forms of cooperation (UN and its specialised agencies, Council of Europe, OECD, OSCE), and where the HR and the Commission are instructed to implement this. These are all (with the exception of some UN agencies) cases where the EU is only an observer, whereas in terms of political realities it is a major participant.

It may be argued that there may at times or even often be little difference between an enhanced observer or virtual member status compared to full membership. While this is surely valid for many 'soft-dialogue' meetings where no decisions are taken, these categories of second-class status can amount to practical disadvantages, for example when real policy orientations have to be agreed, or when the leadership of an organisation needs to form a steering group with restricted membership.

The statutes of organisations admitting the REIO and RIO categories also set out precise rules for how the EU and member states may vote. The general model is a hybrid one, in which either the EU alone or the member states may vote, but not both, and where the EU votes, it carries the number of votes of all the member states taken together (see Box 3 for details). It is usually to be complemented by a declaration on behalf of the EU and its member states in which the division of competence is clarified.

Box 3. Treaty texts referring to the EC/EU as a Regional Economic Integration Organisation (REIO) or Regional Integration Organisation (RIO)

FAO, Amendments to the Constitution and the General Rules of the Organisation to allow for Membership by Regional Economic Integration Organisations **(**27 November 1991)

Article 11 (extracts)

3. The Conference may by a two-thirds majority of the votes cast, provided that a majority of the Member Nations of the Organization is present, decide to admit as a Member of the Organization any Regional Economic Integration Organization meeting the criteria set out in paragraph 4 of this Article, which has submitted an application for membership and a declaration made in a formal instrument that it will accept the obligations of the Constitution as in force at the time of admission.

4. To be eligible to apply for membership of the Organization under paragraph 3 of this Article, a Regional Economic Integration Organization must be constituted by Sovereign States, a majority of which are Member nations of the Organization, and to which its member states have transferred competence over a range of matters within the purview of the Organization, including the authority to make decisions binding on its member states in respect of those matters.

> **International Coffee Agreement** (11 December 2001)
>
> *Article 4. Membership of the Organization (extracts),*
>
> 3. Any reference in this Agreement to a Government shall be construed as including a reference to the European Community, or any intergovernmental organisation having comparable responsibilities in respect of the negotiation, conclusion and application of international agreements, in particular commodity agreements.
>
> 4. Such intergovernmental organisation shall not itself have any votes but in the case of a vote on matters within its competence it shall be entitled to cast collectively the votes of its member states. In such cases, the member states of such intergovernmental organisation shall not be entitled to exercise their individual voting rights.
>
> 5. Such intergovernmental organisation shall not be eligible for election to the Executive Board under the provisions of paragraph 1 of Article 17 but may participate in the discussions of the Executive Board on matters within its competence. In the case of a vote on matters within its competence, and notwithstanding the provisions of paragraph 1 of Article 20, the votes which its member states are entitled to cast in the Executive Board may be cast collectively by any one of those member states.
>
> **UN Convention on the Rights of Persons with Disabilities** (13 December 2006)
>
> *Article 44 - Regional integration organizations*
>
> 1. "Regional integration organization" shall mean an organisation constituted by sovereign States of a given region, to which its member States have transferred competence in respect of matters governed by the present Convention. Such organisations shall declare, in their instruments of formal confirmation or accession, the extent of their competence with respect to matters governed by the present Convention. Subsequently, they shall inform the depositary of any substantial modification in the extent of their competence.
>
> 2. References to "States Parties" in the present Convention shall apply to such organisations within the limits of their competence. ....
>
> 4. Regional integration organizations, in matters within their competence, may exercise their right to vote in the Conference of States Parties, with a number of votes equal to the number of their member States that are Parties to the present Convention. Such an organisation shall not exercise its right to vote if any of its member States exercises its right, and vice versa.

Could the RIO model be used more widely in political organisations such as the UN General Assembly and its various agencies? It is in fact invoked in the draft Resolution submitted in September 2010 to the UNGA (but not yet accepted) to enhance the EU's participation rights (see further section 6.1.1 below). The difficulty here is that in the wider domain of political affairs, the objective test of competence may be harder to establish than in the economic domain, or at least that the contours of the core EU competences may be far less obvious in the absence of a hard core of exclusive competences in these domains. Most member states of the UN either do not want to open a floodgate for a large number of currently observer organisations of the UNGA whose objective qualifications may be very thin, or may wish to secure higher status for those organisations of which they are members (for example ASEAN, the African Union, the Shanghai Cooperation Organization, Gulf Cooperation Council, Arab League, etc.). Yet, as the current experience of the EU in the UNGA is showing, other interested parties may block the claims of the EU if their own aspirations are not met. However the principle of eligibility of other RIO cases should be welcomed since comparable regional integration movements in other continents would be positive for the world order.

Documentary data bases. What is lacking so far is a systematic review of the status quo and the presentation of a coherent rationale for the progressive strengthening of the EU's external presence in line with its competences. This is what the present project aims to do. Fortunately there are excellent documentary data bases facilitating the task of analysts:

- *Treaties Office Data Base of the European Commission.*[8] This lists no less than 649 bilateral treaties and 249 multilateral treaties entered into by the European Communities/Commission, summarising in 2 pages each the contents of the Treaty and the precise status of the European Communities/Commission, and whether these are instances of exclusive competence or mixed agreements. This also supplies electronic links to the full texts of the treaties. It also lists the 37 international organisations where the EU has been a contracting party (excluding the UN agencies where it is only in most cases an observer).
- *Inventory of the European Community Participation at the United Nations.*[9] This specifies the present status and competencies of the European

---

[8] Accessible at http://ec.europa.eu/world/agreements/default.home.do

[9] Working Document of European Commission, DG External Relations (Relex).

Communities/Commission in 85 UN institutions, conferences, conventions, agencies and related organisations.

- *Agreements Database of the Council of the European Union.*[10] This offers information on the ratification status of the EU agreements with third countries and international organisations, and gives access to the full text as published in the Official Journal.

---

[10] http://www.consilium.europa.eu/App/accords/default.aspx?lang=EN&cmsid=297

4. Hybrid Combinations of the EU & Member States in International Relations

4.1 Categories

The huge set of international treaties, conventions and semi-institutionalised fora which the EC (now the EU) has acceded to or has some stake in sees in practice several models of formal representation and informal relationships, generally of a hybrid character involving both the EU and its member states.

A first distinction must be made between the cases of formal legal status and power structures within organisations (the vertical relationships), versus less legally formalised but cooperative relationships between autonomous organisations (the horizontal relationships). The vertical and horizontal can be either complementary or alternatives, as examples below will show.

Vertical relationships. More precisely, in the vertical governance structure of international organisations and conventions of international law, the contracting parties of the international agreements become members (or shareholders, or contracting parties) of the legal entity or act. The vertical power structure is two-way: the contracting parties govern the organisation or convention, while accepting to implement various legally binding obligations.

There are several graduations of status seen in practice in the presence of the EU and member states in international organisations and conventions:

- MS may all be members contracting parties, or only some may be members, or they may be absent except as controllers of the mandate of the EU (actually the Council controls the mandate of the EU in all international negotiations); or

- The EU may be full member or contracting party, or ordinary observer, or enhanced observer (virtual member) or absent.

Many but not all of the combinations arise in practice, which we will illustrate below. The cases where the member states act alone in their sovereignty and the EU is completely absent become now a rarity. The reverse case where the EU is the principal party and the member states are absent is mainly limited to technical bodies. This in turn means that the larger part of the EU's international relations consists of hybrid cases, where both the EU institutions and the member states are present in various combinations, often with complex and potentially burdensome arrangements for their coordination, both in respect of negotiations concerning specific agreements and in respect of the day-to-day representation of the Union and its member states. We will review these different types below, since any attempt to reform the system will have to work painstakingly through this complex political and legal landscape.

Horizontal relationships. Horizontal relationships are to be understood as cooperative arrangements between autonomous partner organisations, including both joint actions and softer processes of information exchange and policy dialogue, which may become important even where the partners may have no vertical status in each other's organisation (this is highly relevant for the EU in several instances, as we shall see).

Important relationships of this type have emerged in the case of several international organisations where the EU's operational relationships are substantial, but where it either has no 'vertical' status at all (NATO, World Bank) or has only some observer status (IMF, UNDP, Council of Europe). Typically these relationships see periodic meetings between the leadership of the Commission (together in some cases with the Council Presidency, and now post-Lisbon the HR), and the President/Managing Director/Secretary General of the partner organisation, supported by meetings of senior officials. The high-level meetings may produce Memoranda of Understanding framing the way for operational coordination.

These arrangements are far easier to develop, avoiding the tricky legal and political problems that arise with questions of formal status.

These are also meetings where the EU institution(s) deal alone with the partner organisation, avoiding the problems of meetings unduly burdened with large numbers of member states' representatives.

A question that follows is whether these relatively informal horizontal cooperative arrangements can work effectively in the absence of formal 'vertical' relationships, or whether they should best be complementary. In this respect there is the important distinction between those relationships where the EU and another organisation are collaborating over operations only in 3rd countries (World Bank, UNDP), versus those where the 'other' organisation is intervening in the EU itself or its member states (IMF, Council of Europe). The case for the EU coming into the vertical governance structures of the partner organisations would be stronger in the latter case.

4.2 Guidelines for representation of the EU and member states

Given the huge mass of multilateral agreements and relationships that the EU has entered into, and the variety in the combinations of presence of the EU and the member states, there have to be some basic principles to order the system. For this purpose, the first reference should be the EU's legal order and the Articles of the Lisbon Treaty defining the gradation of EU competences (as set out in section 2 above) and their application by specific sector, although the measure of the real competences of the EU is often a far more complex affair than these treaty articles seem to imply. At least these provisions can give some structure to the EU's overall strategy. When it comes to negotiating the inclusion or revision of the EU's place in various organisations, there will always be the organisations's own statutes that may be more of less easily adapted to the EU's needs and requests. Most of these statutes in relatively old organisations reflect the simple old world of sovereign states, which is why reform to accommodate the EU as a special case is often difficult and requires careful preparation and solid support from the member states in securing the needed diplomatic consensus or adequate majority votes.

The guiding principles could be the following:
- In cases of exclusive competences, the EU would be the pre-eminent actor with full membership of the organisation, or contracting party, while the member states may also (but not necessarily) be present as members, but usually without an independent role. Here the EU

representative would be the Commission, since there are no exclusive competences in the foreign and security policy field.

- In cases of shared competences, and in respect of the foreign and security policy, the norm would be for the EU and the member states both to be members or contracting parties to international agreements. But the shared competences come in many gradations in their legal character and the relative weights of functional responsibilities of the EU and the member states.

    Where the organisation takes operational decisions affecting the Union, or involves legal obligations that fall at least partly into EU competences, or profits from significant EU funding, the case is strongest for full parallel membership of the EU and the member states.

    For organisations dealing with relatively soft processes of coordination, the requirements for adequate representation of the EU can be less demanding than where there are legally binding obligations, or financial implications. For these organisations the status of 'virtual member' or 'enhanced observer' for the EU may be adequate, alongside 'full' membership by the member states, as long as there are full rights for the EU to intervene in debate and present EU common positions and proposals. This avoids complicated formal matters of budgetary contributions, which may be of trivial importance, and of voting rights.

- In cases where the EU has some but only weak competences, it would be an ordinary observer.

A first screening of international organisations and conventions according to the categories of EU competences (exclusive, shared, supplementary, etc.) is presented in Table 1. From this it can be seen that the list of the EU's shared competences is extremely long, which is why the organisation of the hybrid presences of the EU and its member states is a substantial question.

4.3 Overview of the status quo and looking ahead

We now sketch the application of these principles, summarising the main features of the status quo and identifying cases where the status quo has become unsatisfactory, and where a plausible change in the model of representation can be identified.

We start with the two polar and simplest categories, where in the first case the member states are members or contracting parties and the EU is absent, and in the second case, the EU is a member or contracting party and the member states are absent.

MS present, EU absent. The cases where the member states operate without any EU presence is now becoming quite rare. This is because of the huge growth of EU regulatory competences in internal market and justice and home affairs in the past two decades, which have become matters of shared competences. It is striking to note here the key words 'internal' and 'home' affairs, i.e. *not* external affairs. What has turned out in practice is that these enhanced domestic competences of the EU have spilled over into its foreign policy obligations, or the need for consistency between its domestic and international regulatory policies. In the past, these hardly counted as foreign policy matters at all.

Still there are a few very important cases where the EU has no institutional status, including the UNSC, NATO and the World Bank. However, the EU's activity in these fields has spawned the development of limited horizontal relationships, which are described in detail below. In the UNSC, the EU begins to have some limited right to speak, which may now develop usefully, but this has still a weak and precarious legal and political basis. EU-NATO relations have become quite intense over the last decade, starting from zero, and the relationship is now described as a strategic partnership; this could well be enhanced now by reciprocal observer status (at the North Atlantic Council and EU Political and Security Committee). The World Bank situation is a big anomaly, since the EU is now a bigger aid donor than any of its member states and its operational partnerships with the Bank in the European and African regions are important, yet it has not even observer status on the executive board (only on its ministerial policy committee).

EU pre-eminent. At the other end of the spectrum are the cases where the EU has exclusive competences and therefore a pre-eminent position in the relevant organisations and legal conventions. The major case in point is in the trade policy field, concerning the WTO and WCO (World Customs Organization). For the WTO in particular, the EU (Commission) is sole negotiator, operating under mandate from the member states. While these mandates are basically negotiated in Brussels, the member states nonetheless maintain expensive watching missions in Geneva, with officials from all 27 lined up behind and listening to what the Commission says and reporting back home. A single note-taker from the Council Secretariat could suffice and save a lot of money. Also in this category of exclusive competences and roles for the EU are the many international commodity agreements that are adjuncts to trade policy.

It is not so common for the member states to withdraw from organisations or conventions to cede the place entirely to the EU, since inertia or reluctance to give ground is a strong trait. It is also not self-evident for them to do so, as in many instances some of the activities of the international organisation still concern areas where they have some residual competence. However, when the exclusivity is established, cases do arise where the EU's entry into an agreement leads to an 'instruction' for one or more member states to withdraw formally. A case in point was the (admittedly quite esoteric) Convention for Inter-American Tropical Tuna Commission to which the EC acceded in 2006, with Spain having to withdraw.

The other major exclusive competence of the EU is for monetary policy in the eurozone. Here the outstanding anomaly is the eurozone's inadequate representation on the Executive Board of the IMF, where the ECB has only a limited observer status. As detailed below, this anomaly combined with the over-representation of the member states to reach in October 2010 a political crisis point, with the member states being confronted effectively by both the BRICs and the US. The logical future should see a single eurozone seat or constituency. The member states have acknowledged this only for the long-term future; the recent G20 agreement on IMF reform announces 2020 as the next review, which could be a good target date for establishing a single eurozone seat. Another important monetary organisation, the central bankers club at the Bank for International Settlements (BIS), has successfully accommodated both enlargements to include new economic powers and a full role for the ECB.

MS and EU together. The most complex situations arise for the large category of policies that are shared competencies for the EU, where both the EU and the member states have significant presences. Here the EU presence spans a wide spectrum from the 'simple observer' alongside many others (e.g. 67 in number at the UNGA), to the 'enhanced observer' or 'virtual member', and to the full member or contracting party alongside the member states. In general the EU strategy can work steadily towards an upgrading of its presence along this spectrum where the importance of its competences justify this, and member states may come to economise in their representation where this becomes disproportionately expensive or cumbersome. We highlight here three cases or types that are detailed below.

The UNGA is now the flagship case of where the EU languishes with an inadequate observer status, its representatives having much to contribute on many items of the huge agenda that the Assembly regularly treats. Pre-Lisbon, the rotating Council Presidency could intervene for the EU, but as a sovereign state it could do this with full status. Post-Lisbon, it is for the HR (Catherine Ashton) or President of the European Council (Herman van Rompuy) to represent the EU, but procedurally neither of them can properly do this with the EU's status of ordinary observer, with the result that the representation by the rotating Presidency is still a fallback option in those circumstances where the arcane rules of the UN otherwise preclude effective participation of the EU. The EU therefore tabled in September 2010 a draft resolution to enhance its rights for participation in most functional respects, but without the formal status of a member state. As explained below, this proposal has so far failed to pass. If adopted the Resolution would extend these rights to the EU's presence in the UNGA's Committees, Working Groups and UN Conferences, and so the proposal is of extensive significance. It seems likely that this proposal will be re-tabled in the next few months, and may with more thorough explanation and diplomatic lobbying be passed. If it fails again, this will be the signal for a tougher and more strategic approach, drawing attention to the EU's major role as financial contributor to the UN and its agencies and programmes, and demanding a *quid pro quo* if the over-representation of member states elsewhere (e.g. at the IMF) is to be reduced.

Three European or Euro-Atlantic institutions were singled out in the Lisbon Treaty for 'appropriate forms of cooperation', without it being stipulated precisely what that should mean: OECD, OSCE and Council of Europe. In the case of organisations engaged in relatively soft diplomacy the EU already has (OECD), or quite easily can develop (OSCE), the position of 'virtual member', i.e. full functional rights to participate, without however a vote or 'member state' status. The arrangements for EU representation in international organisations is generally being revised now in line with the Lisbon Treaty provisions. While arrangements will differ between organisations, the case of the OECD (for details, see Box 6 in section 6.2.1 below) may be viewed as a template for the relatively simple situation where the status of the EU within the organisation does not change, but the coordination and speaking arrangements do. These arrangements are currently deemed transitional since they retain a residual and temporary role for the rotating Council Presidency to assist the EU delegation pending its reinforcement. On the other hand, the case for upgrading the EU's status at the Council of Europe to full member, rather than just observer, is now precipitated by accession of the EU to the Convention of Human Rights. Since the EU will be now subject to the jurisdiction of the European Court of Human Rights as all member states of the Council of Europe, it should be entitled fully to enter into the governance of the Council of Europe, inter alia as member of the Committee of Ministers.

In the case of organisations and conventions where significant EU shared competences are involved there is a solid case for parallel full membership by the EU and the member states. The modalities of organising this have been worked out in quite a number of cases. The leading example has been that of the FAO, where the EU has very substantial agricultural competences, but which are not exclusive of member states' policies. The EU's role in the FAO is defined in a complex governance structure. According to the individual agenda item at any meeting the EU side indicates whether it is a matter of member states' or EU competence, and this determines who speaks, and when there is voting whether the member states can vote individually and the EU does not vote, or the EU casts a single vote with a weight of 27, and the member states do not vote. On paper the FAO model looks well developed for the situation, yet one hears complaints that it involves excessively heavy procedures and sees insufficient discipline on the side of the member states in observing these rules. These issues warrant a more thorough investigation to see how working practices can be improved.

There are other more recent organisations where both the EU and the member states are contracting parties and/or full members (EBRD, Energy Charter Treaty, Energy Community Treaty, etc.), and where no changes are needed in the EU's institutional position.

On the other hand there are several older organisations where the EU has substantial competences that have not followed the FAO or these other models. These include for example the International Maritime Organization (IMO) and International Civil Aviation Organization (ICAO) where regularisation of the EU's status from observer to full member is long overdue, and where lack of support from various member states is to blame. In these and other examples the EU can invoke the Regional Integration Organisation (RIO) criterion with a view to requesting an upgrade from 'virtual' to full member.

There can also be increasing recourse to informal core group processes within organisations, such as the 'Friends of the UN Secretary General', or 'Green Room meetings' at the WTO. However for this it is important that the EU has full status (as at the WTO), whereas in other organisations where the EU is only observer (UNGA, OSCE, OECD) the Secretary General may find it awkward to invite the EU to such restricted meetings.

One instance of the member states giving way to sole EU membership, with the member states to remain only as observers, has been seen in the Northern Dimension programme when it was restructured in 2007 after its initial decade of experience. This model might be applied in other cases to lighten the costs of large meetings and enhance efficiency.

The exceptionally important case of the G20, which has become a prime forum for global economic affairs, may prove to be too unwieldy to be an effective forum for negotiation. Many different formats can be imagined for handling global issues in more restricted fora, in which case the EU will be under pressure to represent itself alone, without even the larger member states. This would require, however, that the member states would be willing to be represented by the EU (HR or the Commission) also on matters of national competence. For example there could be a remodeled G8 (with US, EU, Japan, the BRICs and South Africa), or a quadrilateral forum (US, EU, China, India) or a trilateral (US, EU, China, or US, EU, Russia). There are already many bilateral summits for 'strategic partnerships' where the presidents of the European Council and Commission represent the EU alone without the presence of the member states. The 'Copenhagen moment' at the December 2009 climate change summit should have served as part of a learning process for the EU and its member states to understand together when it is vital for the EU to be represented with a truly single voice, or to find itself side-lined.

Constituency arrangements. Finally, an issue running through many organisations is the obsolescence of the constituency arrangements in the executive boards or steering groups, where the large member states have their own executive directors and votes, whereas the smaller member states are grouped in constituencies with a single executive director, with voting weights also increasingly out of line with global realities. Aside from the question of voting power, many constituency arrangements are obsolete with regard to the enlargement of the EU and dissolution of the Soviet Union, as in the IMF Executive Board where Canada represents Ireland, and Belgium represents Belarus. Also in the UN system (starting with the UNSC, but also at the UNDP and other agencies), there are executive board arrangements with regional groups reflecting still the Cold War division of Europe, with a so-called 'Western Europe and other States' group and an Eastern Europe group covering the former Soviet bloc. On the other hand the EBRD offers an up-to-date model: the constituencies for smaller member states are separately grouped into EU and non-EU states, and the EU itself (represented by the Commission and the European Investment Bank) has full shareholder and Executive Board status alongside the member states. In principle the constituencies for smaller member states should now be grouped for EU member states, or in the IMF case for eurozone and non-eurozone member states, but the issues involved in such reforms inevitably get tied up with wider global issues going far beyond the EU's internal concerns. Still, when these wider reforms become possible, the EU should factor in its concerns.

5. Restructuring of European Diplomatic Services

5.1 Setting up the European External Action Service (EEAS)

One of the key innovations of the Lisbon Treaty lies in the external representation of the Union, where new positions and structures, as well as the legal personality of the EU, have the potential to lead to a qualitative upgrading of the EU's foreign policy role. The Treaty sees several actors representing the EU. The President of the European Council represents the EU internationally 'at his level', for instance at summits, and provides the strategic guidelines for foreign policy. The President of the Commission and individual Commissioners continue to represent the EU externally on all matters of EU competence except activity under the Common Foreign and Security Policy (CFSP), with the Commission thus remaining responsible for activity under the old European Community competences.

However the High Representative for Foreign and Security Policy, Catherine Ashton, holds the central position. She heads the EEAS, chairs the Foreign Affairs Council and also serves as Vice-President of the Commission. Given the intensity of these multiple obligations, the post has evidently to be supported by deputies at the political as well as technical level. Three Commissioners can represent her in matters pertaining to their portfolios (Stefan Fule for the EU Neighbourhood, Andris Piebalgs for Development, Kristalina Georgieva for International Cooperation, Humanitarian Aid and Crisis Response), while for CFSP matters the HR can delegate to the foreign minister of the rotating Council Presidency, or its other Troika or Trio (following) Presidencies.

The rotating Council Presidency is no longer mentioned in the Lisbon Treaty as playing a role in the EU's foreign policy. However it remains important in chairing other formations of the Council that decide negotiating mandates for external issues in areas of EU competence other than foreign and security policy. It is not yet clear how far the rotating Presidency is 'out' of external affairs activity. The Spanish Presidency of the first half of 2010 clearly did not consider itself 'out', but this was a transitional period, whereas the Belgian Presidency in the second half of 2010 sought to minimise its role in external affairs, beyond standing in for the HR when asked to do so, or when unavoidable for formal reasons (e.g. at the UNGA). The very large network of Council Working Groups will in the CFSP field be chaired by members of the EEAS. The Belgian rotating Council Presidency has continued to chair these working groups while declaring that this was "on behalf of the High Representative", pending the full operational establishment of the EEAS. The Belgian Presidency prioritised getting the new Lisbon structures in place, including the withdrawal of the rotating Presidency from external representation except for temporary transitional arrangements. However the two next Hungarian and Polish Presidencies are taking a more assertive attitude to the functions of the rotating Presidency, and are effectively looking for grey areas in EU institutional rules that may provide ways to re-introduce its role. Some other member states, notably the UK, are taking every opportunity to resist any upgrade in the EU's external role, including even very small pragmatic steps of protocol, like having the EU representation of the Commission and Council Presidency at the Cancún climate change sitting behind a single 'EU' nameplate (see section 6.1.11).

Throughout 2010, the institutions and the member states have spent much energy on the complex negotiations to create the new European External Action Service (EEAS), which became operational on 1 December 2010. The long-term potential of the EEAS is very positive for EU integration: by pooling national and EU officials, tools and resources for EU foreign policy and by bridging what has so far been a political and institutional gap between supranational and intergovernmental institutions, the EEAS could help create a 'foreign policy culture' which could contribute to addressing some of the shortcomings of EU performance in international affairs. In the short term, however, prospects are far more uncertain and will depend also on the extent to which the member states will invest, with people and resources, in a more common and coordinated foreign policy. Indeed, its form and functioning will be reviewed within one year of its establishment, in time also for the negotiations of the next Multi-Annual Financial Framework from 2013.

The deal reached in July 2010, followed by the finishing touches agreed upon during the autumn entails the creation of the EEAS as an autonomous structure from the Council and the Commission, in which most of the staff dealing with foreign policy and external relations will merge. From the Council Secretariat, 411 staff members are to be transferred from its Directorate General for External Relations, the Policy Unit, and most of its CSDP and crisis management structures; from the Commission 1,114 staff members are to be transferred from its Directorate General for External Relations (DG Relex) and part of the Directorate General for Development. However Commission staff responsible for managing financial instruments, in EuropAid, DG Development and ECHO, will not be transferred. Some 100 new posts should be created by 2011, making a total 1,643 staff, of which 1,145 will be of administrative (AD) grade, although this seems now subject to doubt as a result of various inter-institutional arguments. In addition there will be 2,077 staff of other categories, mainly locally employed staff taken over from the former Commission delegations, making a total establishment of 3,720. A budget of €476 million is proposed by the HR for 2011 for staff, administrative and infrastructure, i.e. excluding the EU's operational expenditures, which are of a much higher magnitude (€12 billion).

At the staff level (see the provisional organigramme in Figure 1), the HR will have one deputy in the person of the Executive Secretary-General (French diplomat, Pierre Vimont), who in turn will have two Deputies (former head of Solana's Policy Planning staff, Helga Schmidt, and Head of Cabinet of the President of the European Parliament, Maciej Popowski), respectively in charge of political and inter-institutional affairs. Together with the Chief Operating Officer (former Commission Director General for Trade, David O'Sullivan), these four posts plus the HR will form the 'corporate board' of the EEAS, to use the official terminology. Below the corporate board, the EEAS is organised in directorates-general, five of which focus on geographical areas, one is responsible for multilateral and thematic issues, and one for administrative, staffing and budgetary matters. Further units deal with Crisis Response and Operational Coordination, Crisis Management and Planning, and the EU military staff.

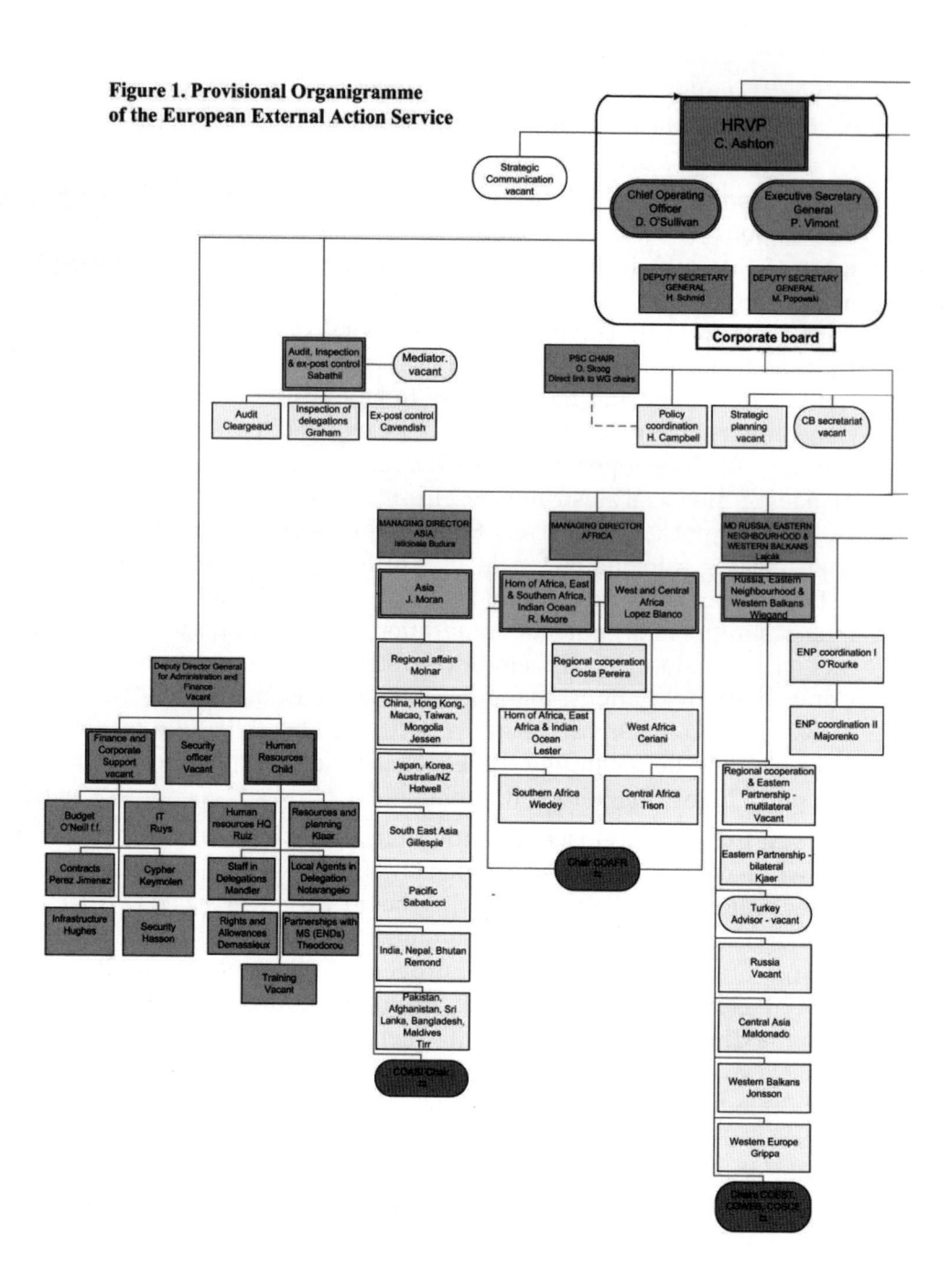

Figure 1. Provisional Organigramme of the European External Action Service

Organizational Chart

Chair EUMC — H. Syren

Counsellor — R. Cooper

MD CRISIS RESPONSE & OPERATIONAL COORDINATION — A. Miozzo**

EUSRs

- EP and national parliaments — Mathiessen
- Legal affairs — Vacant
- SITCEN — Salmi

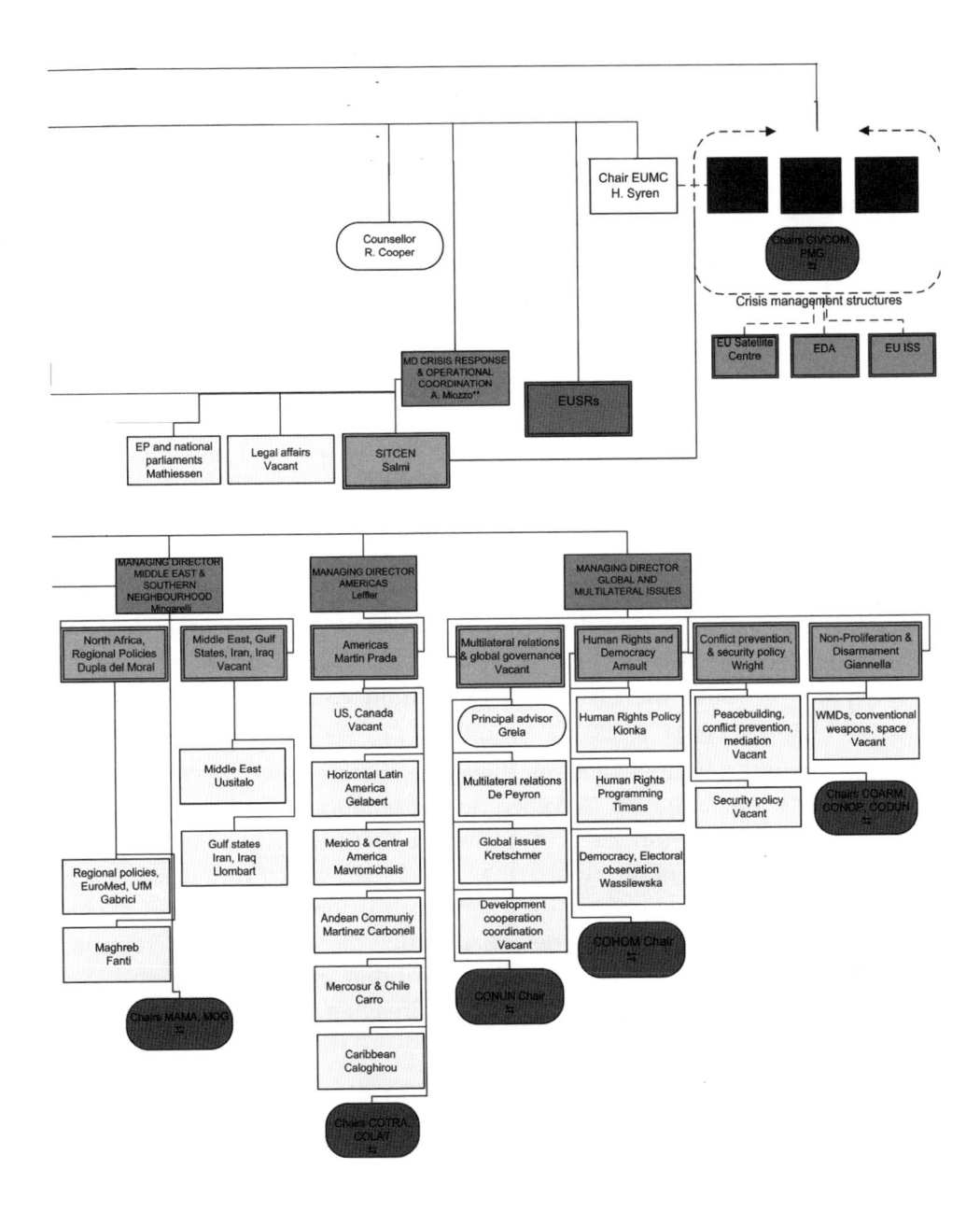

Crisis management structures
- Chairs CIVCOM PMG
- EU Satellite Centre
- EDA
- EU ISS

MANAGING DIRECTOR MIDDLE EAST & SOUTHERN NEIGHBOURHOOD — Mingarelli

- **North Africa, Regional Policies** — Dupla del Moral
  - Regional policies, EuroMed, UfM — Gabrici
  - Maghreb — Fanti
  - Chairs MAMA, MOG
- **Middle East, Gulf States, Iran, Iraq** — Vacant
  - Middle East — Uusitalo
  - Gulf states Iran, Iraq — Llombart

MANAGING DIRECTOR AMERICAS — Leffler

- **Americas** — Martin Prada
  - US, Canada — Vacant
  - Horizontal Latin America — Gelabert
  - Mexico & Central America — Mavromichalis
  - Andean Community — Martinez Carbonell
  - Mercosur & Chile — Carro
  - Caribbean — Caloghirou
  - Chairs COTRA, COLAT

MANAGING DIRECTOR GLOBAL AND MULTILATERAL ISSUES

- **Multilateral relations & global governance** — Vacant
  - Principal advisor — Grela
  - Multilateral relations — De Peyron
  - Global issues — Kretschmer
  - Development cooperation coordination — Vacant
  - CONUN Chair
- **Human Rights and Democracy** — Arnault
  - Human Rights Policy — Kionka
  - Human Rights Programming — Timans
  - Democracy, Electoral observation — Wassilewska
  - COHOM Chair
- **Conflict prevention, & security policy** — Wright
  - Peacebuilding, conflict prevention, mediation — Vacant
  - Security policy — Vacant
- **Non-Proliferation & Disarmament** — Giannella
  - WMDs, conventional weapons, space — Vacant
  - Chairs COARM, CONOP, CODUN

For representation abroad, the Heads of the 136 EU Delegations, substituting those of the Commission, are accountable to the HR, and take over the coordinating role on the ground, which had so far been carried out by the embassy of the member state holding the rotating Presidency – potentially a far-reaching change. In principle the Delegations should develop a key role in articulating EU policies towards third countries, linking not only to the EEAS in Brussels but also to Commission directorates general responsible for sectoral policies with important external aspects (e.g. agriculture, aid, trade, transport, energy migration).

This coordination role will be especially important in the centres of multilateral diplomacy (New York, Geneva, Vienna, etc.). As is detailed in the next section there is a large agenda for the possible expansion of the responsibilities of the Delegations compared to those of the member states, starting for example with rationalisation and reduced duplication of information gathering and reporting.

The system of Special or Personal Representatives of the HR for various regions or conflict situations is currently being reviewed, and likely to be slimmed down, partly in view of the enhanced status of the EU delegations, where the Heads of Delegation could take on the roles of Special Representatives.

There are evident tensions between the member states and the EU institutions over the EU's place in international affairs in terms of competition for resources and influence between the national foreign ministries of the member states, the new EEAS and Commission. At the time of writing (December 2010), there are disturbing signs of backsliding over full development of the EEAS and the post-Lisbon regime, as illustrated above by uncertainty over the build-up of staffing and the re-invention of the rotating Council Presidency in certain external representational functions.

5.2 The costs of non-Europe and the restructuring of European diplomacy

At the outset the EEAS's total staff of 3,720 is small compared to the diplomacies of three largest diplomatic services of the member states, which are in the region of 12 to 13,000, and comparable to the staffing of the medium-sized member states such as Belgium and the Netherlands (Table 2 and Annex N).

Table 2. Staff and financial resources of European diplomatic services

	27 MS	EU
1. Number of missions (embassies & consulates)	3,164	136
2. Total staff (at home and abroad)	93,912	3,720
- Own nationals	55,441	1,643
- Locally employed	38,471	2,077
- Total staff per head of population	1 per 5,335	1 per 134,677
3. Budgetary costs	€7,529 mil.	€476 mil.
- Costs per head of population	€15	€1
p.m. Aid expenditures (development, humanitarian, etc.)	€53,736 mil.	€12,092 mil.
Total staff, external relations and aid, home and abroad, own nationals and locally employed	(est.) 108,149	5,778
Total cost of diplomacy and aid administration	(est.) €9,647 mil.	€649 mil.

Notes: Data for member states are for 2009; for the EU the figures are as proposed at the end of 2010 for 2011. Staff figures under 2. (with details in Annex N) include MFA and EEAS personnel at home and in foreign missions, but exclude aid administrations, which however are separate from MFAs only in some member states (e.g. UK DFID, Swedish SIDA). Where aid administrators are embedded in MFAs and foreign missions, we have sought data on their number, and in most cases it was possible to excluded them from line 2 above (and Annex N), which aims at representing core diplomatic activity. However this was not possible in all cases, and the EEAS figures include aid staff in the Delegations. Exclusion of aid administrators was also statistically appropriate, as in some cases aid agencies combine administration and operations without it being easily possible to separate the two, the German GTZ being a large-scale case of this practice. Budgetary costs in line 3 (and Annex O for detail) cover staff and other administrative and infrastructural expenditures of MFAs and EEAS at home and in foreign missions, but exclude operational expenditures on aid and major cultural programmes and agencies. The Commission employs 1,484 staff in Brussels on aid activity (in AIDCO, ECHO, that part of DG Development not being transferred to the EEAS) and 574 in DG Trade, which are not included in the EEAS data above. Every effort has been made to extract comparable data from national MFAs or their permanent representations in Brussels. But not all member states have responded to our requests completely and the statistics should only be read as giving broad indications. For detailed data see Annexes N, O, P.

The numbers of administrative grade diplomats is of course much smaller, and the EEAS is planned to start with 1,145 'AD' grade diplomats, i.e. excluding technical and secretarial staff and local agents (this suggests as rule of thumb one in three staff as AD diplomats). The 27 member states together employ almost 94,000 staff in their foreign services, which includes both their own nationals and local agents, the latter account for a little under half of the total. The total staff for the 27 member states is over three times higher than for the US (27,882). The Commission employs additionally 2,058 in 'external DGs' that are not transferred to the EEAS (DG Trade, AIDCO, ECHO, and the part of DG Development not transferred), making a total for EEAS plus the Commission of 5,778 persons. These figures do not include international sections of many other Commission DGs or home government departments of the member states (such as finance, transport, etc.).

The administrative budget of the EEAS of €476 million amounts to just under €1 per capita of the population. The total administrative expenditures of the MFAs of the 27 member states amounts to €7,523 million, or about €15 per capita of the population; the largest member states achieve some economies of scale spending less than this average, whereas the smaller but high-income member states are spending on average over €30 per capita. The EEAS represents 1 staff person per 134,677 heads of the EU population, whereas the member states' diplomacies average 1 staff per 5,335 of the population.

These figures are suggestive of the potential scope for major economies of scale in restructuring European diplomacy, with expansion of the role of the EEAS and economising in national diplomacies, wherever the common service at EU level could replace duplication at the level of the 27 or achieve a greater impact. Of course this depends on which diplomatic functions can effectively be performed by the EEAS/EU on behalf of all member states, to which we return in a moment.

Four scenarios are now described below in order to provide some quantitative parameters for cost-benefit analysis of the possible restructuring of European diplomacy. The first two develop the idea of 'budget neutrality', which has been endorsed by the member states in the Council (but are not presented in Table 3 since they are close to the status quo).

Table 3. Scenarios for restructuring European diplomacy

	Staff numbers			Costs, € million		
	EEAS	MS	Total	EEAS	MS	Total
Initial situation, January 2011	3,720	93,912	97,632	476	7,529	8,005
Moderate restructuring MS -10%, EEAS x2	+3,720	-9,391	-5,671	+476	-753	-277
=	7,440	85,521	91,961	952	6,776	7,728
Substantial restructuring MS -25%, EEAS x3	+7,440	-23,478	-16,038	+952	-1,882	-930
=	11,160	70,434	81,594	1,428	5,647	7,075

Notes: In 'moderate restructuring' the EEAS is doubled in staff and costs by 2020, while member states' diplomacies are cut by 10%. In 'substantial restructuring' the EEAS is tripled in size by 2030, and member states' diplomacies are cut by 25%. However some member states are currently proceeding with 10-25% cuts much faster, in 3 to 5 years. Therefore the annual profile of net budgetary economies would be front-loaded in keeping with the current national macroeconomic budgetary imperatives. As a simplifying assumption the cost estimates suppose a linear relationship between changes in staff and total costs including overheads; in reality the total cost changes could be either bigger or smaller than the staff changes, depending for example on factors such as whether small diplomatic missions are closed down or only reduced. Given the front-loading of the national budget economies compared to the longer time profile for expansion of the EEAS, one could in principle make a discounted cash flow (DCF) calculation which would give a higher present day value of the net budget economies embodied in the scenarios. This is not done here, to avoid unwarranted impressions of accuracy. The narrative implied by the scenarios is clear enough.

a. **'Minimalist budget-neutrality'.** This imposes a zero-growth constraint on the budget of the EEAS. This would exclude the possibility that the EEAS really develops its capacity, and so amounts to denial of the purpose of the Lisbon Treaty to build up the role of the EU as global foreign policy actor. It is included in our scenarios since it is the closest to what the member states currently appear to be trying to do, although we consider it to be without merit. This ultra-conservative scenario would represent little more than a partial takeover of the EEAS by the member states with no other change in the structure of European diplomacy.

However the Foreign Affairs Council defined its position on budget neutrality in less than precise terms in a Declaration on 15 October 2010, attached to the amendment to the EU budget for establishing the EEAS in the following terms:

> The Council recalls the great importance that the establishment of the EEAS should be guided by the principle of cost-efficiency aiming towards budget neutrality. The concept of budget neutrality should be seen in the context of resources within the EU budget, including when deciding on new premises. It expects a report on an efficiency savings/redeployment plan in 2011 outlining concrete steps to be taken in the short- as well as medium-term to progress towards budget neutrality and should be subject to regular review.

This declaration at least introduces the word 'towards' budget neutrality, which allows for some growth at least in the short-run. However it fails to endorse any long-run build-up of the EEAS. It also ignores the issue of an integrated rationalisation and development of EU and member states' diplomacies. On the other hand the vague reference to the resources of the EU budget seems to leave open the possibility that a growth of the EEAS might be offset by economies elsewhere in the EU budget, which should not be difficult since the EEAS costs only one-third of 1% of the budget total.

b. 'Common sense budget-neutrality'. A simple and more plausible version of this 'budget neutrality' would be to proceed with the expansion of the EEAS with the national diplomats due to be transferred in 2011 to 2013 to occupy one-third of the diplomatic staff of the EEAS (about 370 persons in total), without however their being replaced at home. However it seems that there is little evidence of explicit non-replacement polices being pursued so far.

c. 'Moderate restructuring'. This scenario would see the EEAS progressively strengthened over the next decade, with a doubling of its staff numbers by 2020, raising the total from 3,720 to 7,440, alongside a trimming of foreign services of member states by 10%, or about 9,391 staff. (Table 3). If this were implemented at an even pace throughout the decade it would mean adding around 120 administrative grade diplomats per year to the EEAS, together with proportionate increases in other staff. The initial

2011 EEAS budget requests 100 new administrative grade posts, and so the present scenario could see a roughly constant expansion at this rate, giving time for the new service to consolidate itself, build up staff strength and infrastructure at a manageable pace. As regards the trimming of national foreign offices, it is supposed (in a highly simplified calculation) that all costs are reduced proportionately with staff numbers, which might then yield a useful net budget savings for the EU and national budgets combined of about €276 million. It is possible that the savings would be greater if the economies in member states' embassies had a large number of closures of mini-embassies, i.e. embassies of small member states accredited to small 3rd countries. Many of these embassies have no more than one or two diplomats, yet have to bear full overhead costs of secure offices and communications, residences suitable for diplomatic hospitality and support staff.[11]

d. **'Substantial restructuring'.** Given the sharpness of current needs for budgetary economies and at the same time for the EU to face up effectively to new global challenges, this scenario sees the EEAS further build up at a continuing rate of about 100 diplomats per year in the period 2020 to 2030, resulting in a tripling of the initial staff strength of the EEAS. Alongside this the budgets of the foreign services of member states would be cut by 25% (Table 4). The EEAS would be brought up to a total staff strength of 11,160, which is comparable to the size of the staff currently employed by three largest diplomatic services of the member states (France, Germany and the UK). This staff increase of 7,440 for the EEAS would occur alongside a reduction of 23,747 staff in national diplomatic representations, and could yield a net budgetary savings of about €929 million or more, since economies in mini-embassies would be even more marked than in the previous scenario.

The figures of 10-25% savings is not entirely arbitrary, since they correspond to cuts in national MFA budgets currently being undertaken by many member states. For example Poland is cutting its bureaucracy 10% across the board over two years, whereas the UK announced in October

---

[11] One of the authors discussed the role of the mini-embassy of a medium-to-small member state with its ambassador, who was the one and only diplomat in the mission. He advised that it was very difficult for him to do 'real' diplomatic work, since much of his time was taken up by administrative burdens, including checking the accounts of the consular section.

2010 spending cuts with a 24% real resource savings for the foreign office over a five-year period. France is making cuts of 5%, or 700 personnel, for 2011 alone. Ireland is making a cut of 13.5% for 2011. Austria is making cuts of 10%, and Slovenia of 20% in the next two years. Other member states with very severe budget problems can be expected to make substantial cuts. It is notable that these cuts are being implemented much faster (within five years or less) than the projected expansion of the EEAS.

To summarise, if one supposes a five-year time horizon for the 10 to 25% national budget savings, but a 10- to 20- year time horizon for the build-up of the EEAS at a rate of around 120 administrative grade diplomats per year, then *the net savings per annum in years 1 to 5 would be as follows*:

- *'Moderate restructuring'*: €103 million net savings per annum (+€47 million for EEAS, -€150 million for the member states) and
- *'Substantial restructuring'*: €329 million net savings per annum (+€47 million for EEAS, -€376 million for the member states).

If one looks only at the EU budget, the annual cost increase of the gradual build-up of the strength of the EEAS would be €47 million, i.e. a trivial 0.04% of the total EU budget. While there is now a serious political debate in the Council over whether the aggregate EU budget should be frozen in real terms over the next multi-year financial period, it would not be serious to propose that all detailed lines within the budget should be frozen in rigid, static gridlock.

It should be emphasised that the above budgetary scenarios are only suggesting very rough hypotheses and numbers. A real budget simulation would require a very much bigger investment in research (beyond what our resources allow) into the statistics and financial accounts of the external services of the member states. Yet the scenarios offer a relevant general narrative. There is a huge amount of wasteful duplication going on in the diplomacies of the member states, and the innovations of the Lisbon Treaty invite consideration of how to follow through with serious measures to achieve both economies and greater collective effectiveness. This would be a further episode in the series known in EU circles as 'the costs of non-Europe'.

Given the prominence being attributed now in the EU institutions to political objectives with the 2020 time horizon, one or other of these scenarios might be inserted into the next revisions of the EU's policy statements focused on this date. But what seems to be lacking so far is any inclination on the part of the member states to combine national restrictions with a strengthening of the EEAS, with an integrated approach seeking to obtain greater benefits for the EU and member states together, alongside net cost reductions. The scenarios for building up the strength of the EEAS could be justified with the following ten rationales.

Coordination and leadership. The Lisbon Treaty should bring more coherence and harmonisation in the EU representation in third countries, with the Delegations now representing the 'European Union', not only the 'European Commission' as before. The Heads of Delegation are now required to take on the functions that were up until now undertaken by the rotating Council Presidency, including speaking in the name of the EU in third countries, convening and chairing on-the-spot coordination meetings with the member states' embassies. Delegations servicing clusters of international organisations (New York, Geneva, Rome, Vienna, Nairobi) will need particularly substantial reinforcement, as has been illustrated by the very large temporary reinforcements seen at the embassies of the former rotating Council Presidencies in New York for coordination purposes during their six-month terms (smaller member states have sent reinforcements of 40 to 60 extra diplomats to New York).

Changing profile of strategic diplomacy. Recent years have seen a remarkable expansion of summit level diplomacy, notably with the G20. At the same time the limits of summit diplomacy have been in evidence, certainly in the case of climate change negotiations (failure at Copenhagen to negotiate a global post-Kyoto regime), and the same could be said of trade negotiations (failure of Doha round). This leads into the need for a different mode of 'horizontal' global diplomacy in order to achieve global objectives, in which the EU for its part has to enter into complex negotiations with a large number of important partner states, working often alongside and in sympathy with non-state actors (NGOs, business interests, etc.).[12] The EEAS and the Commission are in principle well

---

[12] For a well-documented account of this new model of diplomacy, see Anne-Marie Slaughter, op. cit. This author draws attention to abundant examples of how the EU has been showing the way in its internal diplomacy and systemic development, but also remarks: "We might thus expect the European Union to support the creation of global government networks. In fact, however, it is the United States that has led the way in supporting these networks at the global level" (p. 265).

positioned to develop this mode of diplomacy, assuming representational questions are sorted out and staffing is brought up to strength. By contrast this is not the kind of diplomacy that the member states, or almost all of them, can be equipped for – to do it at member state level would be hugely expensive as well as confusing for the third parties.

Political intelligence. At the present time, in the most important world capital cities there are 27 + 1 political counselors or entire political sections of EU diplomatic missions compiling 'exclusive' reports on the same subjects to their home capitals, for example on such topics as the implications of the recent US Congressional elections, the next Russian presidency or reform of the Chinese Communist Party. EC Delegations have up until now often had only weak political sections, or none at all in Delegations concerned essentially with development aid. With the injection of one-third of its staff numbers from member states, the EEAS will now be better placed to take up the task of political reporting as a common service for all member states as well as the EU institutions. A key prerequisite of effective political reporting is excellent knowledge of local languages. The recent enlargements of the EU has already brought in a valuable strengthening of Russian language competence in the EU institutions. The EEAS should also be able to draw now on a corps of diplomats coming from the member states skilled in the major non-European languages (Arabic, Chinese, Japanese, Farsi, etc.). It will be up to the EEAS also to organise increasingly effective cooperative arrangements in important foreign capitals to make common use of specific research efforts or intelligence sources of member states' embassies. It is not necessary to propose a black or white scenario here. The larger member states have teams of several diplomats engaged in political reporting in important capitals, and these teams could be slimmed down alongside a beefing up of the EU Delegations.

Economic intelligence. Similarly the classic embassy has an economic section which is concerned with three basic tasks: i) reporting on economic trends, ii) reporting on aspects of trade policy and iii) assisting in support of 'national' commercial interests. Of these the first two are largely tasks that can be entrusted to the EU delegations, with little value added in having this done 27+1 times, as soon as the EU Delegations are staffed up to do this work effectively.

Support for CFSP operations and humanitarian intervention. During the Solana period as High Representative, the EU became the actor of choice for many soft and not-so-soft security missions, including several with mixed civilian and military components (Balkans, Middle East, East Europe, Central Africa, etc.). There are still major challenges to build up these capabilities both in terms of hardware (e.g. for heavy lift aircraft and helicopters) and trained corps of civilian personnel for soft security and rule of law missions. However the political profile and values of the EU make this dimension of its foreign and security policy particularly in need of reinforcement to the point that the EU's actions can gain in visibility and credibility.

Administration of aid programmes. The Commission has taken steps in recent years to decentralise to a high degree the administration of its aid programmes to its delegations (and these staff are counted in statistics of the EEAS). However the overall staffing of the EU's aid programmes are modest compared to the member states that have large aid programmes. The EU's total ODA effort currently amounts to €12 billion per year, compared to around €9 billion each for Germany, France and the UK, with the Netherlands (€5 billion) and Sweden (€3.5 billion) also important donors. The Commission employs 1,484 staff on aid programmes in Brussels, compared to about 2,300 in France or the UK. The Commission thus employs about one-third less staff for programmes which are about one- third larger: or, the Commission has one staff per €8 million of aid expenditures, whereas France and the UK have one staff for about €4 million of aid expenditures.

Common consular services. The provision of common consular services is now becoming an issue with respect to the processing of visa applications for two reasons. First, there are many countries where the member states are far from fully represented and where solutions have to be found. There is a first example in Moldova of a common visa application centre, located in the Hungarian embassy, which is used by 12 Schengen area states (see Annex J for details). The provision of facilities of this type is badly needed in many countries, especially those in the European neighbourhood, Central Asia and smaller states in other continents. *Ad hoc* cooperative systems are emerging elsewhere (e.g. Spain, Belgium and the Netherlands share a common visa service centre in Kiev, where routine administrative work is outsourced to a private company). The Visegrad countries have established a common consulate in South Africa. The second reason has to do with the fact that the rules for issuing short-term visas are now an exclusive EU competence for the Schengen area, and visitors receiving a Schengen visa are free to travel throughout the Schengen area. In this situation, the decision of the individual member state to issue a visa is in any case now a matter of common interest. It would be natural for work of this type to become part of the common services administered by EU Delegations, and this could have a valuable image-enhancing effect for the EU (the Gonzalez Commission for 'project Europe 2030' advocated this under the heading, "Create a unified visa policy and a European consular service within the EEAS").[13] The Lisbon Treaty also provides that the EU should look after its citizens worldwide, which suggests the need for a further category of 'consular' services, for example to organise common relief efforts to evacuate EU citizens in the event of natural disasters (e.g. the 2005 Asian tsunami) or political emergencies.

Role of bilateral embassies. The other side of the coin is the evolution of the functions of the huge network of 3,184 bilateral embassies, missions and consular offices maintained by the member states. What has been happening to the nature of the services that all these embassies really perform, beyond flying the flag? What in particular do the hundreds of bilateral embassies in the matrix of the 27 member states within the EU now do? The main answer heard from member states' diplomats in these postings is that they have to work on the coordination of positions in EU negotiations. But how far can this be justified as an efficient value-adding service? At the top level Heads of State or Government, foreign and finance ministers are meeting every month, in sessions that are usually prepared by COREPER or multiple other meetings in Brussels, including bilateral connections between staff of the permanent representations, who also are the only people who can also keep track of what is happening in the institutions. At the more technical level the specialised knowledge required to advance negotiations or shape coalitions is very demanding (e.g. the details of regulations for financial markets, or genetically modified foods, etc.), which will not normally be part of the in-depth knowledge of diplomats posted in bilateral embassies. Also to be taken into account is the huge displacement of inter-state negotiations to the Permanent Representations of the member states in Brussels and the multiplicity of working meetings of the EU and its member states at all levels.

---

[13] *Project Europe 2020 – Challenges and opportunities*, report to the European Council by the Reflection Group on the Future of the EU 2030, May 2010.

More fundamentally, the very nature of European integration has overtaken the functions of traditional diplomacy, given the huge expansion of personal mobility, communications, cross-country networks and European dimensions to most businesses except the very local and small scale. The intra-European bilateral embassies occupy many fine chancelleries and residences dating back to the Concert of Europe of a century or two ago, and their staffing seems to belong also to an earlier era. To take just one example, in Rome most member states maintain three embassies and missions – to Italy, the Vatican and the UN agencies, all with their separate ambassadors, staffs and buildings. Can the scale of these embassies be justified to taxpayers in these days of extreme budgetary austerity? Sweden here leads the way and, notwithstanding the healthy state of its public finances, has decided to close its embassy to Belgium and merge it into its Permanent Representation to the EU.

Low-cost solutions in the rest of the world. For diplomatic missions in the rest of the world too, the time has surely come to develop ways to exploit the infrastructure of EU Delegations to offer low-cost solutions to the needs for representation for smaller member states in smaller third countries. For example one can imagine the EU Delegations acting as 'House of Europe' centres for mini-diplomatic missions of the smaller member states that might occupy just one or two offices, profiting from common security and other infrastructural elements. With serious development of common services for political and economic intelligence and consular (visa) services, many of today's embassies could be reduced to such mini-embassies embedded in such 'House(s) of Europe', or simply closed. Or there could be more recourse to the accreditation of roving ambassadors resident at home (a technique used by several small member states), and there could be worked out arrangements for such roving ambassadors to benefit from some kinds of support by the EU Delegations. Arranging visits by politicians and high officials is a highly time-consuming task, and one can also imagine arrangements whereby groups of member states without embassies could share a diplomat embedded in the EU Delegation to support such services.

Slovenia (and maybe other small member states) has already expressed interest in the idea of mini-diplomatic representations to be co-located in EU Delegations, but Brussels has so far been preoccupied with basic priorities of getting the EEAS started. The issue could be taken up in the course of the next year.

Political legitimacy. As regards the democratic legitimacy of such a restructuring operation, repeated Eurobarometer opinion polls have shown that EU citizens place a more effective foreign and security policy at the top of their wishes for the enhanced tasks of the EU. This suggests that public opinion, while little informed about the precise mechanisms of EU institutions and policies, has a clear intuition that the EU could and should become a more effective global actor.

6. STATUS QUO & PERSPECTIVES FOR SELECTED INTERNATIONAL ORGANISATIONS, CONVENTIONS, AGREEMENTS & SUMMITRY

This chapter gives an extensive but hardly exhaustive account of the status quo for three groups: first, global multilateral organisations and conventions; second, European and Euro-Atlantic multilateral organisations; and third, less formally institutionalised summitry and other priority diplomatic activities. Where appropriate, we comment on the adequacy or otherwise of the status quo.

6.1 Global multilateral organisations and conventions

6.1.1 UN General Assembly

The EU has the status at the UNGA of one of the 67 'permanent observers', allowed to speak but only after the 192 member states have had their say, although it has sometimes been given a preferential place in seating and speaking arrangements over other observers. The issue of full membership for the EU has been discussed in the past as part of the much wider debate about reform of the UN, and especially of the UN Security Council.[14] The

---

[14] For detailed accounts of UN and UNSC reform, see Natalino Ronzitti, "The reform of the UN Security Council", Documenti IAI 10/13 July 2010, Rome; and Nicoletta Pirozzi, "The EU's Contribution to the Effectiveness of the UN Security

main reservation expressed over an EU upgrade has been over who else would seek to exploit a precedent granted to the EU. The 67 observers include most of the world's official regional or thematic multilateral organisations. Among them the Holy See has secured a prior place with a specific Resolution in 2004 defining its rights as a 'non-member State observer'.

The case for upgrading the status of the EU in the UNGA is robust, both in principle and for some functional reasons. The EU has substantial state-like institutional features, extensive political, economic and legal powers, and since Lisbon, international legal personality. It takes a position on, or has operational responsibilities for, a very large number of UN activities. No other international entity is comparable. An established concept in several international organisations is the Regional Economic Integration Organisation (REIO), permitting such entities to accede to full membership alongside sovereign states. This has been used to legitimise the EC's accession to the FAO and several other multilateral organisations. There is now a precedent case of a Regional Integration Organisation (RIO) clause for one recent UN Convention, i.e. dropping the word 'economic' and making for an opening towards other political or other non-economic organisations.

There is a particular consequence of the Lisbon Treaty that makes the case for upgrading the EU's position urgent. Over the past years the positions taken by the EU on many UNGA matters have often become texts of choice for numerous other UN member states to support. So far these EU positions have always been presented by the rotating Council Presidency state, with a widespread interest in the Assembly for these positions to be tabled early in the contributions of the 192 member states. This task now falls to the EU Delegation. But here there is the practical problem under present rules of procedure that the EU (whichever of the possible representatives just listed) cannot intervene until as many of the 192 UN member states as want to have intervened, which means that the Assembly's work will be made less efficient and the EU's influence reduced.

Council: Representation, Coordination and Outreach", Documenti IAI 10/14, July 2010, Rome.

As a result the EU took the initiative to propose in September 2010 a Resolution of the UNGA (see Annex L for the full text), invoking its regional integration organisation (RIO) status and proposing a comprehensive upgrade of its representative's rights at the UNGA, as follows:

> ... the representatives of the European Union shall be entitled to participate effectively in the sessions and work of the General Assembly (including in the general debate) and its Committees and Working Groups, in international meetings and conferences convened under the auspices of the Assembly, as well as in United Nations conferences. For this purpose, the representatives of the European Union shall have the right to speak in a timely manner, as is the established practice for representatives of major groups, the right of reply, the right to circulate documents, the right to make proposals and submit amendments, the right to raise points of order, and seating arrangements which are adequate for the exercise of these rights.

The draft resolution was tabled at the 64th session of the UNGA on 13 September 2010, where however it encountered objections from various Latin American, Caribbean, African and Arab states who were concerned about how other regional groups would be treated after this precedent. Urgent attempts were made to adjust the text accordingly (as in Annex L), but the next day a vote was taken to postpone the agenda item, which was passed by 76 votes to 71, with 26 abstentions. This means that the issue will have to be tabled again at the 65th session, now underway, with the outcome at present uncertain. The EU believes that no country is against its requests, and that only fuller consultations are needed. Still this episode has seen a serious diplomatic miscalculation on the part of the EU in New York.

If the resolution is finally passed in the near future, this should be a sound basis for many years of progressive deepening of the EU's role in the UN system, both within the UNGA and its subordinate bodies, and as a precedent that could be adopted also in other UN agencies..

Comment: The EU's failure to win support in September 2010 is a setback, hopefully only a temporary one. A lesson from this experience is the need to organise diplomatic lobbying more thoroughly with all UN member states, to which the member states should actively contribute as well as the EEAS.

6.1.2 UN Security Council

Until 1963, only 11 members sat on the UNSC. In December of that year, two measures were adopted. The overall number of UNSC members was raised to 15, and a geographical distribution of seats for the 10 non-permanent members was adopted: five for Asia and Africa, two for Latin America, two for the 'West European and Others' group (WEOG) and one for 'East European states' (EUREST) containing the old Soviet bloc.[15] This division of Europe remains still as a vestige of the cold war, with EU member states now largely present in both of the latter groups, with the result that the EU may now be represented by up to 3 non-permanent seats, in addition to France and the UK as permanent members.

In recent decades, debate over reform of the membership of the UNSC has been a continuous process, with persistent claims for enlargement, but consistent failure to reach consensus.[16] In relation to the status quo of 5 permanent and 10 non-permanent members, there has been a durable G4 bloc seeking permanent membership status (Germany, Japan, Brazil and India), which has gained substantial support, including from France and UK. However this has been opposed by a different G7 bloc, which advocates the expansion of non-permanent membership (Italy, Spain, Canada, Mexico, South Korea and Pakistan). Secretary General Kofi Annan made a proposal in 2005 with two options, both increasing total membership to 24, with different mixes of types of membership.

The competing interests of large EU member states in this process (Germany, Italy, Spain) has led to some debate over whether an EU presence could be part of the solution. The former German Foreign Minister Joschka Fischer when in office suggested that an EU seat would be an acceptable alternative to Germany's accession if France and UK agreed to withdraw, which they do not. For their part the rest of the world is increasingly concerned about the over-representation of the EU in the

---

[15] Resolution 1991-XVIII, adopted on 19 December 1963.

[16] See Ronzitti, op. cit., Pirozzi, op. cit., and David Hannay, "Effectiveness and Ineffectiveness of the UN Security Council in the Last Twenty Years: A European Perspective", Documenti IAI 09/28, November 2009, Rome.

UNSC, with five of the 15 seats (2 permanent and usually 3 rotating) tending to be occupied by EU member states.[17]

While in the long-run there is a case for the EU to replace France and UK, for the time being the way is open to make full use of the provisions of the Lisbon Treaty in Article 34 (TEU), which requires member states who are members of the UNSC to defend the positions and interests of the EU, and in particular states:

> When the Union has defined a position on a subject which is on the UNSC agenda, those member states which sit on the UNSC shall request that the High Representative be invited to present the Union's position.

More generally the EU or member states sitting at the UNSC can as and when it has an agreed position on a specific item on the UNSC's agenda, request permission of the Presidency of the UNSC to intervene in its open debates, which has been the regular practice since the beginning of 2010. This makes use of Rule 39 of the UNSC's Provisional Rules of Procedure, which states:

> The Security Council may invite members of the Secretariat or other persons, whom it considers competent for the purpose, to supply it with information or to give other assistance in examining matters within its competence.

On 4 May 2010 HR Catherine Ashton made her first statement to the UNSC on the subject of cooperation between the EU and UN in the area of peace and security. Another recent example of the EU's partial presence in the UNSC's activity has been in the case of the Iran sanction issue. The sanctions agreed on 9 June 2010 (UNSC 1929) were agreed by the so-called E3+3 (France, Germany, UK, + China, Russia, US), 'with the support of the High Representative of the European Union'. The HR was moreover mandated by the E3+3 to continue dialogue with the Iranian counterpart with a view to finding a solution (see Annex J).

---

[17] "This level of over-representation ... is likely to become increasingly unacceptable to other countries over time, especially as the Lisbon Treaty takes effect and the EU defines a stronger CFSP", according to John Van Oudenaren in "Effectiveness and Ineffectiveness of the UN Security Council in the Last Twenty Years: A US Perspective", Documenti IAI 09/30, November 2009, Rome.

Ideas for partial reform of the UNSC could involve the merger of the two WEOG and EUREST groups into a single European group with a reduction of the number of seats from 3 to 2 (and with the 'other' non-European states to join the groups for the American or Asian continents). In the new European group there could be a seat for the EU itself. In October 2010 Portugal made a proposal upon its new accession to the UNSC as a non-permanent member for two years, writing to the HR to propose that its delegation at the table of the UNSC could include a representative of the EU, presumably either the HR or the Head of Delegation in New York. This interesting proposal awaits a response.

Comment: Arrangements provided in the Lisbon Treaty for the representation of EU positions in the UN Security Council offer opportunities for the time being for the HR/VP to intervene on behalf of the EU where common positions are adopted. While a comprehensive reform of the UNSC remains a huge political challenge, intermediate solutions may be envisaged to encourage coherence among EU member states and reinforce the role of the EU itself at the UN.

6.1.3 *International Monetary Fund*

The IMF is a special case for the EU with its work blending a major 'exclusive' monetary policy competence for the eurozone with a 'shared' competence (with the requirement for coordination) for economic policy at the EU and member state levels.

Membership of the IMF for the eurozone and European Central Bank can be justified on legal and functional grounds.[18] Article VIII of the IMF Agreement sets out obligations of member states regarding current and capital payments regimes and reserve asset policies. These obligations can no longer be fulfilled entirely or at all by the member states of the eurozone. Article IV provides for official consultations on monetary policies, which necessarily involve the ECB in consultations over any single eurozone state. The IMF statutes allow for member states that have formed monetary unions to pool their representation on the Board. But if the monetary union's representative were to be additional to the member

---

[18] For a thorough review see Der-Chin Horng, "The ECB's Membership in the IMF: Legal Approaches to Constitutional Challenges", *European Law Journal*, Vol. 11, No. 6, November 2005.

states, this would require a special agreement of the Board or Governing Council.

At present, neither the Commission, the rotating Council Presidency nor the eurozone finance ministers' group has any formal representation on the Executive Board of the IMF, but the ECB is an observer for agenda items of relevance to it. However the Commission participates as observer in the meetings of the IMF's and World Bank's 'Joint Ministerial Committee of the Board of Governors on the Transfer of Real Resources to Developing Countries' ('Development Committee').

There are two outstanding related issues concerning the Executive Board: first the constituency system for smaller states and voting weights, and second the presence of the EU/eurozone. At present there are obsolete groupings of EU and non-EU states in various constituencies, with Spain grouped with several Latin American states, and with Belgium and the Netherlands grouped with mixed collections of Balkan and East European states (see Annexes D and F). The Commission proposed to the Council in 1998 and again in 2006 reform of this anomaly with groupings of EU member states together, but member states in the Council have proved conservative, refusing such reforms. However, in 2006, the European Council did pronounce itself in favour of a single eurozone/EU seat or constituency "in the long-term". Several years ago France and Germany seriously considered merging their representation on the Executive Board, which could have provided the core for a eurozone constituency, but the idea was dropped. In the event of a eurozone constituency, it would be natural for the positions of director to be occupied by the ECB and for the alternate director to be filled by a eurozone ministry of finance, probably that of the chair of the eurozone group, or the Commission.

The EU member states have been under increasing pressure in the G20 to accept a diminution of their voting weights and seats. As Table 4 illustrates, the EU 27 have a weight double that of the US, and over three times bigger than the BRICs taken together, whereas the EU's economic weight is already less than that of the BRICs and relatively declining fast, and by 2020 may have dropped to half that of the BRICs. The G20 agreed in principle at Pittsburg in June 2009 to make an adjustment of voting weights to transfer 5% of the total in favour of emerging and developing economies by the November 2010 G20 summit meeting in Seoul, which would mean catching up with what the World Bank did earlier in 2010 (see also Table 4).

Table 4. Voting weights in the IMF and World Bank, and GDP shares

	IMF, voting weights on board, %	World Bank, voting weights on board, %		GDP, % of world, est. 2010 at p.p.p.		
year		Pre-2010	2010	2010	2015	2020
EU 27	32.0	28.5	26.3	20.8	18.7	16.6
US	16.7	16.4	15.8	20.2	18.3	16.4
Brazil	1.4	2.1	2.2	2.9	2.8	2.7
Russia	2.7	2.8	2.8	3.0	3.0	2.9
India	1.9	2.8	2.9	5.2	6.1	7.0
China	3.6	2.8	4.4	13.3	16.9	20.6
BRICs total	**9.6**	**10.5**	**12.3**	**24.4**	**28.8**	**33.2**

Note: For the World Bank, the old and new numbers relate to before and after the revisions made in 2010.
Source: IMF, World Economic Outlook database, April 2010, for 2010 and 2015. For 2020 the trend changes over the period 2000 to 2015 is extrapolated for the five further years.

These issues came to a boil in September 2010 when ongoing discussions over revising the Executive Board's structure before the November G20 Summit in Seoul reached an impasse. The US declared that it would not agree to renew the mandate of the Board unless its membership would be reduced from 24 to 20, with European states expected to account for the reduction. The default situation threatened by the US if no agreement were reached was that the Board would be automatically reduced to 20 members with withdrawal of the smallest voting shares. As the Brazilian executive director has pointed out, this would mean evicting Argentina, Brazil, India and an African constituency.[19] The US thus chose to play its cards for Europe to bear the obvious diplomatic costs of such a scenario, in implicit alliance with the BRICs. Meanwhile the EU argues in favour of a broad revision of IMF governance issues, including de-monopolisation of the position of the managing director by Europe on condition that the US agrees to the same for the World Bank, reduction of the voting majority threshold to eliminate

---

[19] P. Noguira Batista, "Europe must make way for a modern IMF", *Financial Times*, 24 September 2010.

> *Box 4. G-20 Communiqué of Finance Ministers and Central Bank Governors on IMF reform, 23 October 2010 [extract]*
>
> We have reached agreement on an ambitious set of proposals to reform the IMF's quota and governance that will help deliver a more effective, credible and legitimate IMF and enable the IMF to play its role in supporting the operation of the international monetary and financial system. These proposals will deliver on the objectives agreed in Pittsburgh and go even further in a number of areas. Key elements include:
> - shifts in quota shares to dynamic EMDCs and to underrepresented countries of over 6%, while protecting the voting share of the poorest, which we commit to work to complete by the Annual Meetings in 2012.
> - a doubling of quotas, with a corresponding roll-back of the NAB preserving relative shares, when the quota increase becomes effective.
> - continuing the dynamic process aimed at enhancing the voice and representation of EMDCs, including the poorest, through a comprehensive review of the formula by January 2013 to better reflect the economic weights; and through completion of the next regular review of quotas by January 2014.
> - greater representation for EMDCs at the Executive Board through 2 fewer advanced European chairs, and the possibility of a second alternate for all multi-country constituencies, and
> - moving to an all-elected Board, along with a commitment by the Fund's membership to maintain the Board size at 24 chairs, and following the completion of the 14th General Review, a review of the Board's composition every 8 years.

the effective veto power of the US, as well as downward revision of European voting weights.

Confronted with this US position, the EU member states agreed to negotiate, and this produced the outcome at the G20 finance minister's ministerial on 23 October 2010, whose institutional aspects are reproduced in Box 4.

The EU member states agreed to cede two seats on the Executive Board. While the details remained to be fully-worked out, it seems that the 'two seats' are to be made up by four advanced European states ceding each a fraction of their seats by agreeing to a rotation with others. Belgium, the Netherlands and Switzerland are expected to cede half their seats, and Spain one-third of its seat by agreeing to a three-way rotation (with Mexico and Venezuela).[20] In addition it is understood that there will be a wider revision of the constituency system, which should present the opportunity for a rationalisation in the direction of EU and/or eurozone constituencies. However some contrary tendencies seem to be in play, with Spain to rotate with non-European states and France bidding to lead a new constituency with a mix of other EU and non-EU European states, in which case Germany and the UK may do the same. Details of the redistribution of voting weights are not yet fully available. However 6.4% of voting weights will be redistributed to underrepresented member states in total, with China due to see its weight increase from 3.65% to 6.39%.

There is EU coordination on the spot in Washington, but with a double problem of proper articulation of the EU/eurozone position, first, when the EU Council Presidency is not a Board member, and secondly now after Lisbon when the EU (in this case the Commission, or ECOFIN Council Presidency, or eurozone presidency) should take over this role from the rotating Presidency, but does not have even observer status on the Board.

In addition the Commission, ECB and IMF have continuous 'horizontal' working relations at all levels, from Managing Director/President/Commissioner to lower staff levels, and there is extensive and growing operational coordination between the IMF and the EU over many joint financing operations, both for aiding third countries (e.g. in Eastern Europe) and now over the Greek crisis and the trillion dollar joint EU-IMF package of measures worked out in response. These working relations are said to be smooth and constructive.

Comment: The system of IMF governance is under sustained pressure for reform, including a revision of voting weights and seats in the Executive Board to cut the overrepresentation of the EU member states in favour mainly of the BRICs. In October 2010, the US joined in ratcheting up this pressure, forcing EU member states to make concessions. However the status of the EU and ECB is still unsatisfactory, with only partial observer status for the ECB and none for the EU or eurozone (finance ministry) leadership. For the longer-term the European Council has acknowledged the case for a single EU/eurozone seat or constituency. The case for a single eurozone seat is imperative if the EU is to punch its weight in

---

[20] Press reports suggest that Belgium, Switzerland and Spain are reconciled to their concessions, whereas the Netherlands is withholding its agreement.

international monetary affairs, without which the member states condemn themselves to continuing divisions and failure to deliver effective messages.

6.1.4 World Bank

The EU is not represented on the Board of the World Bank even as observer (but see above regarding the Development Committee), notwithstanding its major role in development aid and policies, with similar anomalies as in the IMF over constituencies and voting weights, although the World Bank has been able to implement some revision of voting weights in 2010. Although the Board rarely votes, the issue is of high political sensitivity (for example when the US voted against proposed projects in Tibet, China withdrew the projects in question). The Development Commissioner participates as Observer in the World Bank Development Committee.

The constituency system in the Executive Board suffers, as in the case of the IMF, with politically obsolete groupings of countries, and could be reformed by minimally grouping EU member states together. In addition the EU should itself become at least a permanent observer. The case for a single EU seat is less compelling than in the case of the IMF for the eurozone, but the double pressure to reduce member states' representation and enhance that of the EU will continue to mount.

There are on-the-spot coordination meetings of the EU member states' Executive Directors in Washington (every week), with resulting EU positions expressed so far by the Executive Director from the rotating Council Presidency. It remains to be clarified who will represent the EU now post-Lisbon. In principle it should be the EU Delegation, but this is at present impossible, given the absence even of observer status.

On the other hand there is a lot of structured operational cooperation between the World Bank and the Commission, with several memoranda of understanding (MoUs) signed to frame various regional cooperation programmes. Operational partnerships go way beyond these procedural MoUs, and concern World Bank operations in some new member states (Romania), the non-EU states in the Balkans and the countries of the European Neighbourhood Policy. In all these cases the World Bank seeks explicitly to support EU strategies, or more generally 'Europeanising' actions. For example in the Romanian case the World Bank's projects to advance Romania's efforts to meet the EU's strategic 2020 objectives are being financed out of EU Structural Funds.

Comment: The status quo is unsatisfactory in the Executive Board, with obsolete constituency groupings and without proper representation of the EU. In the short-run the constituency system should be revised and the EU should enter as a permanent observer; a single EU seat would be logical at some future point, depending on how political pressures from third countries develop.

6.1.5 Food and Agriculture Organization (FAO), IFAD and WFP

Initially the EEC was an observer at the FAO, until the organisation adopted a REIO clause to its Constitution, allowing the EEC to accede in 1991 as full member. For this the EEC made a declaration of its exclusive and shared competences in the FAO domain. At each FAO meeting the EU or member states have to indicate who has competence and who shall exercise the right to vote with respect to each agenda item; this depends on a heavy procedure for decisions by the relevant Council working group in Brussels. When the EU votes on matters of its competence it has the number of votes of all member states together. In cases of exclusive competence the Commission expresses the EU position, in accordance with a mandate of text agreed at the relevant Council Working Party. In cases of shared competence, the EU position has in the past been expressed by the rotating Council Presidency, with both the member states and the Commission being allowed to speak in support of the common position. The FAO model is quite sophisticated and well specified, but criticisms are heard over its complicated procedures and the lack of discipline on the part of representatives of the member states in respecting these procedures.

But the post-Lisbon situation is uncertain, with the Commission saying that it should now be the sole spokesperson on exclusive and shared competences, while member states' diplomats are arguing that Lisbon changes nothing, and that the role of the rotating Council Presidency should remain. After long discussions a 'transitional' arrangement has been used in the second half of 2010, under which the EU is a single team sitting behind the EU nameplate, with the Commission speaking on exclusive competences and a Belgian diplomat speaking on shared competences (but on behalf of all 27, not the Presidency, nor Belgium). This transitional arrangement has been necessary in any case as a means of compensating for the understaffing of the EU Delegation in Rome, which should be corrected in 2011. This 'team' arrangement has nothing to do with the 'team' mentioned in Article 218.3, and has no sound legal basis.

Also in Rome, along with the FAO, are two other UN agencies working on related topics: the International Fund for Agricultural Development (IFAD) and the World Food Programme (WFP). Unlike in the case of the FAO, the EU is not member but only observer in IFAD and WFP, despite being a major financial contributor to both. Various member states led by the UK (in the second half of 2010) resisted the implementation of the Lisbon Treaty for the Commission to represent the EU on the grounds of its limited observer status. This illustrates why these status questions can hardly be evaded.

Comment: The FAO model for EU representation pre-Lisbon is a seriously structured solution for the case of a complex organisation where both the EU and the member states are full members, and where the EU has a mix of exclusive and shared competences. However the detailed implications of the Lisbon Treaty are not yet fully worked out. The situation in IFAD and WFP sees the EU with a lesser observer status only and currently unresolved dispute over representational prerogatives, despite the fact that the EU is a major funder of these organisations.

6.1.6 *International Labour Organization (ILO)*

The EU is an observer at ILO, while all member states are members. EU-ILO cooperation dates back to an agreement of 1958, establishing the modalities for cooperation and mutual technical assistance. At that time, no specific agreement was reached on the formal status of the EEC at the ILO.[21] Cooperation has intensified gradually, in line with the development of EU competences and responsibilities. In 1961, a Permanent Contact Committee was set up, providing for meetings between the ILO Deputy Director-General and the European Commissioners for External Relations and Social Affairs, as well as officials. In 1989, the EEC was granted observer status at the ILO. By an exchange of letters, the parties agreed that the Commission would be regularly invited to attend the meetings of the Governing Body.[22]

Comment: The ILO adopts conventions which set rules for employment, social policies and migration policies, and which bear directly on EU legislation in this field. On this basis membership along the lines of the FAO model would be

---

[21] http://www.ilo.org/public/english/bureau/leg/agreements/eec.htm

[22] http://www.ilo.org/public/english/bureau/leg/agreements/eec3.htm

appropriate, but this would require amendment of the constitution of the ILO to permit the participation of REIOs.

6.1.7 UNCTAD

The EU is an observer at UNCTAD, which meets in plenary ministerial session once every four years, with its Trade and Development Board meeting at senior official level every 6 months. UNCTAD has seven thematic working groups and there the EU is able to participate as a virtually full participant.

Comment: In view of its major competences in both trade and development fields, it is anomalous that the EU is not a member alongside the member states.

6.1.8 UN Development Programme (UNDP)

The EU has substantial operational dealings with the UNDP, both for coordination of development policies and projects on the ground, and with the Commission in quite a number of cases contracting the UNDP to execute its own projects. The member states are all members, and the EU an observer. The Executive Board is made up of 36 states, organised in 5 rotating regional groups, of which the group "Western Europe and other States" has 12 places of which 6 are currently EU member states and otherwise includes Australia, Iceland, Japan, Norway, Switzerland and the US. There is also an Eastern Europe group that currently includes Russia, Serbia and Slovakia.

Comment: In view of its operational dealings with UNDP, the EU should be member alongside the member states, which would first require recognition of a role for REIOs in the UNDP framework. In addition the constituency system is an obsolete relic of the cold war period with its division between Western and Eastern Europe (as is also the case with the whole UN system).

6.1.9 Development cooperation

Development cooperation is a shared competence, but of a special type sometimes called 'parallel competences' (TFEU, 4.4), according to which both there may be a common policy without prejudice to the right of the member states to conduct their own policies. In practice both the EU and the member states are executing large aid programmes.

Cotonou Agreement. The flagship instrument for the EU's development policy is the Cotonou Agreement concerning the relations between the EU and 78 African, Caribbean, and Pacific (ACP) states. The agreement was established in 2000 and runs to 2020 with revisions every five years. It replaced the previous five-year agreements called the Lomé Conventions, first negotiated in the 1970s. The negotiation round concerning the latest revision was concluded in March 2010. The contracting parties are the EU and the member states on the one hand and the ACP countries on the other.

The Commission has thus far represented the EU and the member states in these negotiations relating to revisions of the Cotonou Agreements. This was also the case with the preceding Lomé Conventions. The Commission's role in these negotiations is however not due to an exclusive competence to do so, but rather has primarily been a matter of tradition.

Who will represent the EU in the coming negotiations on Cotonou revisions, and further ahead in its successor is not etched in stone, and it is possible that the HR will take on this role wearing her Commission hat.

From a financial perspective, Cotonou is almost exclusively about development. However, the agreement also includes important political aspects, such as the possibility to enter into consultations with ACP states in case of deterioration in the internal political environment. Furthermore the legal basis for the conclusion of these agreements is not the part of the Treaties having to do with development but the article for entering into association agreements. This also reflects the more contractual approach to development that supplanted the earlier emphasis on economic aid. An important part of Cotonou is the Economic Partnership Agreements (EPAs) which are essentially free trade agreements formulated as a part of an overarching development strategy.

A peculiarity in this context is the European Development Fund (EDF), which is the main financial instrument of the Cotonou Agreement. While development policy has since long been a shared competence between the Community and the member states, the EDF itself is not part of the EU budget but is set up as an intergovernmental fund whose management is entrusted to the Commission. The relative contributions to the fund by the member states are connected to their history as colonial powers, with in particular France being one of the biggest donors. Attempts, by primarily the Commission, to make the EDF a part of the EU budget has so far been unsuccessful due to several factors. While a member state like France would have to contribute less, it would also lose influence over how the funds are used. Member states like the UK, Italy or newer

Central European members would on the other hand have to increase their contributions considerably. A 'budgetisation' of the EDF would also give the European Parliament a greater say in these issues.

The frontier between development and foreign and security policy. A small but highly sensitive case has arisen over the European Commission's contribution to an action of the Economic Community of West African States (ECOWAS) to limit the proliferation of small arms and light weapons. The Commission argued that this was a matter of development policy and therefore in its competence, whereas the Council argued that it was a matter of security policy. The Commission took the case to the European Court of Justice, which ruled in 2008 in its favour. From the perspective of the Commission the ruling was an instance of the jurisprudence catching up with practical reality of the development programmes it administrated. For the Council and several of the member states, this was regarded as a virtual declaration of institutional war.

With the new competences of the HR under the Lisbon Treaty, this distinction may be less important, but it illustrates how there may be demarcation issues between the HR and the Commission over who is to represent the Union. A general consequence of the Court ruling seems to be that a pragmatic and problem-oriented approach that generally characterises development programme financing has had to give way to a strict, and one could argue, slightly artificial separation between the policy goals of peace and security on the one hand and development on the other. This essentially means that in drafting proposals in the area of CFSP, the Council will be extremely careful to never mention the word "development" in describing the aims of the proposal.

Comment: The EU's institutional position is strongly established in the field of development policy, with the Commission as sole negotiator upon mandate of Council. There may be demarcation issues between the HR and Commission to be clarified.

6.1.10 UN Environment Programme (UNEP)

Current preparations for negotiation of a global convention limiting the discharge of *mercury* into the environment is providing a test case for how the EU should be represented externally in areas of shared competences. In June 2010 there was the start of UNEP negotiations in Stockholm on a globally binding instrument on mercury for the years 2010-13. Within the EU the competence for environmental matters is shared between the Union and the member states. Decisions over the mercury case could be a precedent for other instances of shared competence. The contracting parties in the mercury case will no doubt be both the EU and the memer states. However it was not clear who would negotiate.

The Commission interpreted the Lisbon Treaty as requiring that it should be the sole EU negotiator on all issues in the UNEP negotiations over mercury. The Council contested this, and after lengthy discussions agreed to a compromise, namely to give the Commission the lead on all issues except for two ('financing' and 'capacity building'), where the rotating Council Presidency would lead. However this Council compromise was then rejected by the Commission, claiming that the Council acted illegally, basing its case on Article 17 of the Lisbon Treaty, which reads: *"With the exception of the common foreign and security policy, and other cases provided for in the Treaties, it [the Commission] shall ensure the Union's external representation."* The Commission subsequently withdrew its proposal for the mandate for the negotiations. The Council for its part challenged the Commission's actions, saying that the Commission does not have a right to withdraw its mandate proposal once the Council took a decision. As a result there emerged the prospect of the case being taken to the European Court of Justice to decide the matter; either the Commission would take the Council to Court, or vice versa. In the meantime at the first session of the conference in Stockholm, the Commission had to declare that there was no EU position: a classic instance of inter-institutional wrangling spilling over into the international arena.

Fortunately this impasse did not last and on 6 December 2010, the Council was able to take a decision in agreement with the Commission as follows:[23]

> *(1) The Commission is hereby authorised to participate, on behalf of the Union, as regards matters falling within the Union's competence and in respect of which the Union has adopted rules, in the negotiations on a legally binding instrument on mercury, further to Decision 25/5 of the Governing Council of UNEP.*

---

[23] Council of the EU, Decision on the participation of the Union in negotiations on a legally binding instrument on mercury further to Decision 25/5 of the Governing Council of the United Nations Environment Program (UNEP), 16632/10, 6 December 2010.

(2) The Commission shall conduct these negotiations on behalf of the Union, as regards matters falling within the Union's competence and in respect of which the Union has adopted rules, in consultation with a special committee of representatives of member states, and in accordance with the negotiating directives set out in the Addendum to this Decision.

(3) To the extent that the subject matter of the agreement falls within the shared competence of the Union and of its member states, the Commission and the member states should cooperate closely during the negotiating process, with a view to aiming for unity in the international representation of the Union and its member states.

This is useful specimen text, since it deals with the general issue of shared competences where in the given policy domain some elements per (1) are strictly of Union competence, and some other elements per (3) are a mix of Union and member states' competences. In the former case the Commission is sole negotiator. In the latter case it remains to be seen who shall represent the member states, alongside the Commission or HR representing the Union. The member states are here entitled to choose who should represent them; it could be the Commission, or the Council Presidency, or one or more individual member states, but with a view to unity. In (2) the member states will support, steer and supervise the Commission through a special committee which is to be presided, as with all non-CFSP Council working groups, by the rotating Council Presidency.

Comment: The current UNEP mercury negotiations have been a test case for clarifying how the EU should be represented in complex shared competences cases. After a phase of inter-institutional conflict between Council and Commission, there has emerged an outcome that looks workable and at least has the merit of removing such internal EU wrangling from the international stage.

6.1.11 UN Framework Convention on Climate Change (UNFCCC) & Kyoto Protocol

Both the UNFCCC and the Kyoto Protocol are matters of shared competence, where both the EU and the member states are contracting parties. At the Copenhagen climate change summit of the UNFCCC in December 2009, the complexity of the representation of the EU and its member states was widely criticised.[24] In Copenhagen the EU was represented by the Troika (the rotating Council Presidency, accompanied by next rotating Presidency and the Commission with assistance by the Secretariat of the Council), with the rotating Presidency in the lead. In the Kyoto Protocol track negotiations, the lead negotiator was the Commission, while in the second track ('Long-term Cooperative Actions' - LCA), there was a team of negotiators under the leadership of the rotating Presidency.[25]

With a view to the then forthcoming Cancún summit in December 2010, the Council under the Spanish Presidency established a new team of negotiators for the LCA track consisting of UK (lead), Poland, France and Germany. In October 2010 more precise preparations for Cancùn at the level of COREPER (part 1) led the Belgian rotating Council Presidency, after substantial debates, to define the following arrangements:[26]

- "the representatives of the Commission and of the Presidency, speaking on behalf of the EU and its 27 member states, would take the floor from behind the 'EU' nameplate",
- "internal coordination would be ensured by the Presidency" and
- "the current practice in international conferences on climate change with a team of lead negotiators and supported by issue leaders and experts charged with the negotiation for the EU and its member states will continue to be the practice throughout the negotiations".

The notable innovation in these arrangements is for the hybrid EU representation to be put together behind the EU nameplate, rather than having the rotating Council Presidency speak from his/her national seat.

---

[24] Piotr Maciej Kaczyński, *Single Voice, single chair? How to re-organise the EU in international organisations under the Lisbon rule*, CEPS Policy Brief No 207, CEPS, Brussels, March 2010.

[25] T. Delreux and K. Van den Brande, *Taking the lead: informal division of labour in the EU's external environmental policy-making*, IIEB Working Paper No. 42, April 2010, University of Leuven (http://soc.kuleuven.be/iieb/docs/wp/IIEBWP042.pdf).

[26] Presidency non-paper of 20 October 2010, "Practical arrangements for external representation of the EU at the 16th session of the Conference of the Parties (COP 16) to the UNFCCC and the 6th session of the meeting of the Parties to the Kyoto Protocol (CMP 6), Cancún", 29 November to 10 December 2010.

Most criticised at Copenhagen was how the informal negotiations in restricted groups of major players developed. There were scenes of several member states leaders and Barroso milling around with Obama and other leaders, and finally the infamous ad hoc meeting between Obama and the group of developing countries which determined the final conference conclusion and communiqué without the presence of any EU representative. If Obama had wanted to be accompanied by just one EU representative at this meeting, he had a large menu of choice over who it should be. At Copenhagen the EU was not lacking in a position of substance, and actually was rather well prepared at the technical level, but its representation at the top political level was a confusing array of personalities. For Cancún the Mexican chair arranged for it to be at ministerial, not summit level, and the outcome was widely considered to be more positive than Copenhagen.

Comment: While it is clear that both the EU and the member states will be contracting parties to any next UNFCCC agreements, the status quo remains complicated on the details of who negotiates for the EU.

6.1.12 World Health Organization (WHO)

The WHO is the only organisation included in this survey whose subject matter – public health – figures in the lowest rank of EU competences, where according to Article 6 (TFEU) the EU engages in actions that are only 'supplementary' to national policies. While this reflects national responsibilities for public health care systems, the EU has significant responsibilities in this field, including the regulation of pharmaceuticals and their advertising, and health and safety standards. It also becomes involved internationally over policies to control global health threats and pandemics. The EU is an observer at WHO. The EU is prominently active in the WHO Euro Regional Committee, which holds an annual ministerial meeting, such as the one in Moscow in September 2010 where the EU Commissioner and his officials were active participants in various ministerial panels and working groups. EU coordination was organised under the transitional post-Lisbon 'joint team' approach, with official EU positions presented by the Belgian Council Presidency.

Comment: While the EU's status as observer is reasonable, the arrangements for it to represent its views in plenary WHO meetings is not yet in line with the Lisbon Treaty provisions.

6.1.13 *World Trade Organization (WTO) and World Customs Organization (WCO)*

WTO. Due to its long established exclusive competences in the trade field, the WTO case is the most developed model of EU representation. The EU is a member of the WTO alongside the 27 member states. The WTO has a complex governance structure, with a Ministerial Conference (not every year), a General Council meeting around 8 times a year in Geneva at ambassador/senior official level, four more specialised Councils meeting at senior official level, and several Committees, Working Groups and Working parties. The general rule is that only the EU speaks and negotiates, while the member states are or can also be present. Positions taken by the EU are prepared at meetings with the member states (in the 'Trade Policy Committee') chaired by the rotating Council Presidency. As an exception to the general rule, member states ministers may speak briefly at the Ministerial Conferences.

The EU Head of Delegation and staff in Geneva are key players in all the WTO fora. There will now be in fact two Delegations in Geneva, one for WTO and the other for UN affairs. This split will allow greater autonomy for the Commission trade policy circuit led by the responsible Commissioner from the foreign policy circuit presided by the HR.

The WTO has in its founding act a 'one country, one vote' rule, but votes are never taken. The member states make the budgetary contributions, not the EU, so they do speak in the Budget Committee.

Given the unwieldy 153 members, there is recurrent use of informal restricted groups, including the UN model of 'Friends of the Chair', in which the chairperson of the various committees invites around 5 to 8 main players, and the Commission will always be in these groups, while the member states will not be. Similarly the Director General convenes so-called 'Green Room' meetings (named after his office décor) of main players in the course of negotiations processes, generally including the Commission without the member states.

There used to be a super-restricted 'Quad' group consisting of the EU, US, Canada and Japan, at which the four 'ministers' (including only the Trade Commissioner for the EU) would meet about twice a year to try and steer global trade policy, but this has now stopped meeting because of its lack of representation of emerging powers. However no new steering group has emerged, given that the G7/8/20 do not get into trade policy matters beyond vague declarations about continuing to pursue the Doha Round.

While the EU's arrangements at WTO are now well tried, they are nonetheless expensive in the extent to which the member states sit silently behind the Commission negotiators in the General Council, most of the main Committees and formal negotiating sessions. The Commission's mandates are generally decided in Brussels at the Council, and for many meetings in Geneva it would seem possible to dispense with the high costs of the proceedings being observed by all or most member states, when one EU note-taker might suffice.

Comment: Overall the EU's presence in the WTO system seems to be stable and to be functioning reasonably smoothly, although the lack of an effective global steering group seems now to be a weakness in the system. The member states incur high and arguably excessive costs in being silent observers of the Commission at many WTO meetings.

WCO. In June 2007, the WCO agreed to the request of the European Community to accede as full member. The decision grants to the EU rights and obligations on an interim basis akin to those enjoyed by WCO members. Full accession will be possible once an amendment to the relevant Convention allowing economic and customs unions to join is ratified by the 172 current members. The WCO works on issues such as harmonised trade nomenclature, customs valuation, rules of origin, harmonisation of customs procedures, etc. The EU was already a contracting party to several WCO Conventions.

Comment: Full membership is pending.

6.1.14 International Maritime Organization (IMO) and related agreements

The EU's presence in maritime organisations has become increasingly topical since 2006 when the Commission published a Green Paper seeking to develop an integrated maritime policy for the Union.[27] The issue of the EU's representation in the several international maritime organisations and conventions was the subject of a detailed study undertaken for the

---

[27] European Commission, *Green Paper - Towards a Future Maritime Policy for the Union: A European Vision of the Oceans and Seas*, COM(20006) 275, 7 June 2006.

Commission at Leuven University.[28] In the three examples that follow it will be noted that one sees the EC/EU represented correctly for its exclusive competence (ICCAT), whereas the other two instances are subject to anomalous treatment (IMO, IWC). In total there are 36 conventions and agencies concerned with maritime affairs, including fisheries and environmental matters (see Annex C). Of these the EU is party alone without the member states in 7 cases, while 19 see the presence of both the EU and member states, with 10 cases where the EU is only observer (including the IMO and IWC, detailed below).

International Maritime Organization (IMO). The IMO is a specialised agency of the UN, with 168 members, entrusted with maritime standard-setting functions (conventions, codes, etc.). It can take binding decisions and is depositary for many international agreements on subjects such as maritime pollution, collisions at sea, liability for maritime claims, etc. In IMO matters the EU generally has shared competence with the member states, and the EU has generated a large amount of legislation directly based on IMO conventions and resolutions.

However the EU has not been represented as such at the IMO and has not acceded to any of its Conventions. Since 1974 the Commission has had observer status. From the formal standpoint this is because the IMO Convention does not have a Regional Economic Integration Organisation (REIO) clause as in the case for example of the WTO, which would permit the EC/EU's accession as member. Since this situation was deemed unsatisfactory the Commission addressed a recommendation to the Council to permit it to negotiate with the IMO adoption of a REIO clause in order to permit the EU's full accession. However the Council has not acted on this, maybe because of blocking positions by member states with large maritime interests (voting weights in the IMO are by tonnage of national fleets). For the time being, EU positions are expressed by the rotating Council Presidency in the name of the member states and the Commission.

International Whaling Commission (IWC). Here the EU has exclusive competence in general for conservation of biological resources under the sea, as explicitly confirmed in the Lisbon Treaty. The IWC

---

[28] Leuven Centre for Global Governance Studies, *Study for the Assessment of the EU's Role in International Maritime Organizations*, Final Report (J. Wouters, S. de Jong, A. Marx, P. de Man), April 2009.

Convention reserves membership for States, and so as in the case of the IMO the Commission is an observer. Again a Commission proposal for full accession to the IWC Convention, addressed to the Council in 1992, has not been agreed. In practice therefore the EU position has been expressed by the rotating Presidency, which is even more anomalous than the IMO case since this is an exclusive competence.

International Commission for the Conservation of Atlantic Tunas (ICCAT). The conservation of tuna enters into an exclusive competence of the EC. The ICCAT Convention of 1966 was originally open only for States, but in 1984 a Protocol opened it to REIOs, and the EC's accession was approved in 1986, and finally entered into force in 1997. The member states withdrew their membership as a result. The Commission speaks and votes on behalf of the EC, in accordance with positions agreed in the Council Working Group on External Fisheries Policy. EC delegations to ICCAT meetings are led by the Commission, accompanied by experts from the member states.

Comment: These three examples reveal two cases (IMO and IWC) where the EU should be member but is only observer, which are anomalies given the importance of EU competences in these areas (even exclusive in the case of the IWC). On the other hand in the case of the ICCAT where the EU also has exclusive competence, the member states withdrew their membership after the EU became full member.

6.1.15 *Bank for International Settlements (BIS) and financial market regulation*

The BIS is the club of leading central banks, which has rapidly extended its membership in recent years from a restricted trans-Atlantic to a global membership. It has 56 member central banks, including most EU member states and the European Central Bank. It has an executive board of 19 members, of whom 6 are permanent members (Belgium, France, Germany, Italy, the UK and the US), with other elected members including the ECB, China, India and Brazil. The BIS has a leading role in formulating standards for banking regulations, such as the successive Basel I and II capital requirements standards. On 12 September 2010, a new Basel III was agreed, tripling the reserve capital requirements of banks in response to the recent financial crisis, after negotiations which were chaired by the President of the European Central Bank. The BIS's role has been especially important for the EU, which legislates the mandatory implementation of the Basel standards as the core of its financial sector regulatory policies. This was illustrated when the Commission announced on 13 September 2010 that it will propose in early 2011 legislation for the EU to implement Basel III.

The BIS is also host to the new Financial Stability Board (FSB), which has been set up by G20 to oversee the adequacy of the regulation of financial markets world-wide after the 2008-09 crisis. The Commission as well as the ECB play full part in its work.

The EU for its part has moved promptly in setting up a much enhanced common regulatory system, namely the European System of Financial Supervision (ESFS), comprising a) the European Systemic Risk Board (ESRB), b) the European Banking Authority (EBA), c) the European Supervisory Authority (Securities and Markets), d) the European Supervisory Authority (Insurance and Occupational pensions) and e) the Joint Committee of the European Supervisory Authorities. The new structure was adopted in EU law on 22 September 2010.[29] The system is authorised (in Article 18 of the regulation governing the EBA, reproduced in Box 5) to develop contacts and enter into administrative arrangements with the analogous supervisory authorities of third countries.

Box 5. European Banking Authority - International relations, Article 18

1. Without prejudice to the competences of the Union Institutions and member states, the Authority may develop contacts and enter into administrative arrangements with supervisory authorities, international organisations and the administrations of third countries. These arrangements shall not create legal obligations in respect of the Union and its member states, nor shall they prevent member states and their competent authorities from concluding bilateral or multilateral arrangements with third countries.

2. The Authority shall assist in preparing equivalence decisions pertaining to supervisory regimes in third countries in accordance with the acts referred to in Article 1(2).

3. In the report referred to in Article 28(4), the Authority shall set out the administrative arrangements agreed upon with international organisations or administrations in third countries and the assistance provided in preparing equivalence decisions.

---

[29] Proposal for a regulation of the European Parliament and the Council establishing a European Banking Authority, 6 September 2010, Interinstitutional File: 2009/0142(COD)13070/1/10 REV 1.

These bodies are effectively EU agencies. They are mandated to represent the EU in external matters within their competence, for example liaising with US regulatory authorities. They do not have powers to take legally binding decisions, but they are entrusted to prepare decisions that will normally be taken by the Commission, for example in recognising the equivalence of the regulatory rules or decisions of third countries.

Comment: More so than at the IMF, both the ECB and the member states are full participants at the BIS. Basel I, II and III standards have successively become the basis for EU legislation drawn up by the Commission and decided with the Council and Parliament in normal legislative procedure. New arrangements for financial market regulation at European and international levels are satisfactory from an EU institutional standpoint. The new set of EU regulatory bodies have been mandated immediately from the start to engage directly in cooperation with the authorities of third countries.

6.1.16 *Other economic organisations and regulatory agencies*

Here we signal a number of instances where EU representation is not in line with its competences.

In the transport sector the civil aviation sector lags behind realities, as was shown to also be the case for the maritime sector.

At the *International Civil Aviation Organization (ICAO)*, the Commission has to ask for observer status for each and every meeting, despite the major significance of EU law in civil aviation market matters, and in international negotiations such as with the US over an open skies agreement.

At the *World Intellectual Property Organization (WIPO)* the place of the EU has evolved positively alongside its growing competence in this area, and it is now regular observer and full participant in three expert committees, but EU positions there are still being presented by the rotating Presidency notwithstanding Article 17 (TEU) which would give this to the Commission.

At the *International Telecommunications Union (ITU)* the EU has observer status, but as for WIPO, would be entitled to negotiate for the EU on at least part of its agenda. Similarly the Commission is observer at the Universal Postal Union (UPU).

By contrast in the *Internet Governance Forum*, which is a multi-stakeholder platform for non-binding deliberations on internet issues, the

Commission has an effective role. This is typical of the situation in new organisations where the role of EU (or Commission) can be more readily brought into line with functional realities than in older organisations where inertia and rigidity of statutes hinder this.

Comment: Old organisations come to terms with growing EU competences only very slowly, and here the internal EU rules for who speaks for the EU in cases of shared competences as between the Commission and rotating Council Presidency (for non-CFSP matters) remain confused in practice.

6.1.17 *International courts*

The International Court of Justice (ICJ) was founded upon the inception of the UN, and all 192 UN member states are *ipso facto* parties to the Statute of the ICJ. It deliberates over disputes between states which have recognised its jurisdiction, and gives advisory opinions on legal questions upon request of the UNGA, UNSC or other authorised UN organs and specialised agencies. Its most recent action of relevance to the EU was the advisory opinion on Kosovo's declaration of independence handed down in July 2010. As principal organ of the UN, the ICJ has no governing assembly of its own. Until now the EU has been represented by the rotating Council Presidency. This does not preclude other member states making submissions of their own. However it should not be difficult in the future for the EU to represent itself directly since the Court or its President may invite "international organisations … likely to be able to supply information on the question" to make submissions (Article 66 of the ICJ Statute). However in contested cases the EU cannot itself act either as applicant or respondent, but only via some member states.

The International Criminal Court (ICC) is far more recent, established pursuant to the Rome Statute of 1998, coming into force in 2002 after receiving sufficient ratifications. At present it has 114 state parties with another 25 that have signed but not ratified. The ICC is mandated to deal with cases of genocide, war crimes and crimes against humanity. In spite of the very large number of states having acceded (in Europe, Latin America and sub-Saharan Africa), China and India are not parties. Russia and the US, while having signed, have not ratified. The US signed under Clinton, but the first Bush administration then took a hostile position, with emphasis on the maintenance of immunity for its armed forces fighting abroad. The US started to cooperate with the ICC during the second half of the 2000s, and has been playing a constructive role under Obama, but is highly unlikely to ratify in the near future.

While all member states are parties to the Rome Statute, the EU has observer status at the ICC's Assembly of the State Parties and the Review Conference, with no right to vote. The EU can make statements or declarations and was represented so far by the rotating Council Presidency (now presumably to be the Commissioner for Justice, Fundamental Freedoms and Citizenship). The EU is committed to the ICC and to promoting the widespread ratification of the Rome Statute, adopting Common Positions on the ICC in 2001-03 and an Action Plan in 2004.[30] Further, the EU and ICC signed a Cooperation and Assistance Agreement in May 2006. In addition, the EU supports the ICC with public statements and declarations, also at the UN. The EU has also funded projects aimed at supporting the ICC's work. The EU has adopted several Decisions to strengthen member state cooperation in the investigation and prosecution of crimes falling within the scope of the Rome Statute.[31] Cooperation with the ICC in fighting genocide, crimes against humanity and war crimes is a priority set out in the Stockholm Programme, the EU's blueprint on JHA for 2009-14.[32]

Comment: In view of the increasing importance of the EU's cooperation with the ICC, its observer status could be enhanced, either in formal terms or at least throught a more active participation in the conferences of the Assembly of Parties.

---

[30] Action Plan to follow up on the Common Position on the International Criminal Court (http://www.consilium.europa.eu/uedocs/cmsUpload/ICC48EN.pdf).

[31] Decision 2002/494/JHA, of 13 June 2002 (OJ L 167/1, 26.6.2002), setting up a European network of contact points in respect to persons responsible for genocide, crimes against humanity and war crimes; Framework Decision 2002/584/JHA, of 13 June 2002 (OJ L 190/1, 18.7.2002), on the European arrest warrant and the surrender procedures between member states; and Decision 2003/335/JHA, of 8 May 2003 (OJ L 118/12, 14.5.2003), concerning the investigation and prosecution of genocide, crimes against humanity and war crimes.

[32] Council of the European Union, 'The Stockholm Programme – An open and secure Europe serving and protecting citizens, 5731/10, Brussels, 3 March 2010.

6.1.18 UNHCR (refugees), Human Rights Council, IOM (migration)

The EU has substantial legal competences and operational relations vis-à-vis the UN High Commissioner for Refugees (UNHCR), the UN Human Rights Council (HRC) as well as the International Organisation for Migration (IOM). The EU has observer status at all three. The EU plays an active role in the proceedings of the UNGA Third Committee (Social, Humanitarian and Cultural) and the HRC, introducing proposals for resolutions and giving statements aiming to protect and promote human rights.[33]

Refugees. The EU has observer status also at the UNHCR Executive Committee (ExCom), which has 79 members, of which 21 are EU member states. The ExCom is tasked with advising the High Commissioner, reviewing funds and programmes, authorising the High Commissioner to make appeals for funds, and approving proposed biennial budget targets. The subject matter of the ExCom's work is either asylum policy, which since the Amsterdam Treaty has become a 1st pillar competence, or humanitarian aid, both of which are shared competences between the EU and the member states.

The primary legal texts are the 1951 Geneva Convention and its 1967 Protocol, which define what the term 'refugee' means and outlines a refugee's rights. A key provision, which has become part of customary international law, stipulates that refugees should not be returned to a country where they fear persecution (principle of *non-refoulement*). In 1999, the EU launched a process towards the creation of a Common European Asylum System (CEAS), based on the legislative harmonisation in the area of asylum and refugee protection. The completion of the CEAS remains a key policy objective for the EU under the Stockholm Programme,[34] which foresees the EU's accession to the 1951 Convention and its 1967 Protocol, subject to a report from the Commission on the legal and practical consequences of its accession, expected in 2013.[35] In the meantime the

---

[33] See European Communities (2004), *The Enlarging European Union at the United Nations – Making Multilateralism Matter*, Brussels.

[34] Council of the European Union, The Stockholm Programme - An open and secure Europe serving and protecting citizens, 5731/10, Brussels, 3 March 2010

[35] European Commission, Action Plan Implementing the Stockholm Programme, COM (2010) 171 final, Brussels, 24.4.2010.

substantive protection of the 1951 Convention and 1967 Protocol is guaranteed by the European Court of Justice for matters of asylum and immigration within the scope of EU law.

While the EU has observer rights at the ExCom, the EU's ability to exercise its competences in full is limited, since observers are for example unable to make proposals or participate in the negotiation of its conclusions on key policy questions. This inconsistency should be corrected in the short- to medium-run by the granting of full participant status.

Human rights. The UN has recently sought to reinforce its work in the human rights area, creating in 2006 the UN Human Rights Council, as successor to the Commission on Human Rights. The Council conducts a periodic universal review of the human rights record of all UN member states. The Council has 47 members, with the following geographical distribution: Africa 13, Asia 13, Eastern Europe 6, Latin America and Caribbean 8, and Western Europe and 'other' 7. Of two European groupings, 7 are currently from the EU member states. The Council is criticised for a debilitating politicisation of its actions. The EU has not been able to exercise leadership there, although the member states have in most cases been 'speaking with one voice' on the Council. As a minority group on the Council the EU has been caught between being isolated or opting for consensus-building with other states. The latter choice, which has been increasingly the EU's preference, has meant a watering down of the content of EU-sponsored resolutions.

Migration. The subject matter is a shared competence. The EU's observer status at the IOM is very limited, and applies only to annual Council meetings, with no right to attend the Standing Committee on Programme and Finance. The issue of EU membership was sounded out informally in 2009, and not pursued in response to uncertainty whether there would be sufficient support to make the necessary change in the statutes.

6.1.19 Arms control – conventions and organisations

In 2003 the EU adopted a Strategy against the Proliferation of Weapons of Mass Destruction, which is the framework for a large number of actions concerning principally:

- the Biological and Toxic Weapons Convention (BTWC),
- the Chemical Weapons Convention (CWC),

- the International Atomic Energy Agency (IAEA) and
- the Comprehensive Nuclear-Test-Ban Treaty Organization (CTBTO).

The EU is not a contracting party to these conventions, or member of the organisations, but has become a significant operational partner through the adoption of numerous common positions, joint actions and decisions under the CFSP. The most recent progress report on the WMD Strategy lists the 10 Common Positions, 20 Joint Actions (with budget support mostly in the range of €1 to €7 million each), and 14 Council Decisions or Regulations, and 21 Projects decisions and projects costing in total about €330 million.

The Biological and Toxic Weapons Convention is not supported by an international organisation to oversee and enforce treaty compliance. The States Parties therefore meet ad hoc, but with regularity, and in particular the periodic quinquennial 'Review Conference'. There are also annual meetings at expert and political levels known as the inter-sessional process.

At the 2006 Review Conference, EU officials were an integral part of the rotating Council Presidency delegation (Finland). The Common Position was presented by Finland on behalf of the EU. In addition, EU member states had prepared technical working papers, which were presented by the member state on behalf of the EU, and had a powerful impact. It became the practice for the Presidency to make a statement on behalf of the EU, with EU officials (Council and Commission) sitting with the Presidency delegation.

Since the entry into force of the Lisbon Treaty, there has been one meeting of experts in August 2010 as part of the current inter-sessional programme. Belgium, as the current rotating Council Presidency, has adopted the principle of the Presidency Team, with emphasis on EU officials rather than on the Presidency. Thus, the EU representative in Geneva read an EU statement from the Belgian seat, while the summaries of the working papers were presented by an EU official from the benches reserved for *observers*. Belgium made no country statement on behalf of the EU. With respect to the forthcoming 2011 Review Conference, Belgium has placed the centre of gravity for the preparations with the Directorate 'Non-Proliferation and Disarmament Issues' within the General Secretariat of the Council and the future External Action Service.

The Organization for the Prohibition of Chemical Weapons (OPCW) comprises all the State Parties to the CWC. It consists of three bodies: the

Conference of States Parties (CSP), the Executive Council (EC) and the Technical Secretariat headquartered in The Hague. The Conference of the States Parties (CSP) is the highest decision-making body of the OPCW. The Executive Council (EC) is composed of 41 states parties, which rotate on a two-yearly basis, with membership distributed over geographical regions, with representation assured for a number of states with the most important national chemical industries.

Presently, the EU has no representative to the OPCW, without even observer status. So far EU statements have been presented by the rotating Council Presidency (who however may not always be seated on the Executive Committee), with EU officials joining the Presidency delegation in order to participate in the meetings. How it will work post-Lisbon is not yet clear.

Comment: The status quo arrangements for the EU's presence in the WMD organisations or processes have lagged behind its increasing substantial activity in this field. Worse still, the post-Lisbon rules for the HR to replace the rotating Council Presidency will be frustrated unless the EU is granted at least an 'enhanced observer' status in these organisations or processes.

6.2 European and Euro-Atlantic multilateral organisations

6.2.1 OECD and IEA

The status of the EU in the OECD and its many committees and working parties is officially 'observer', but an agreement provides for the EU to be as if a member for most practical purposes alongside the member states. In the Trade and Agriculture Committee only the Commission speaks, but in all other committees the EU and the member states may intervene. The EU does not contribute to the budget. The case for full membership can be based on the substantial EU exclusive or shared competences in almost all of the OECD's committees, and could be reinforced by recourse to the REIO principle as in the UN system.

While the EU's status at the OECD is hardly an issue, there is still the separate question – as in many organisations – how the EU organises its coordination and representation. The work of the Belgian Presidency of the second half of 2010 to clarify the post-Lisbon regime is instructive here. In this as in other cases Belgium sought to manage the transition to the post-Lisbon regime with a view to helping the HR and EU Delegations perform their new functions in spite of the fact that the EEAS had not yet been fully established. In particular Belgium sought to confirm the withdrawal of the rotating Presidency from representing the EU, rather than fight a rearguard action to re-invent its role, which some other member states seem to favour. The details of the arrangements are given in Box 6.

> *Box 6. EU Coordination and representation in the OECD, in implementation of the Lisbon Treaty*
>
> **Coordination.** The EU Delegation will organise and chair, with the support of the Belgian Permanent Delegation where appropriate, coordination meetings at the level of Ambassadors, deputies, committee level, or by issue. Meetings will be convened at the initiative of the EU Delegation or at the request of a member state or the Commission. These coordination meetings will aim at exchanging information and identifying common positions where possible and/or required. The Belgian Permanent Representation will assist the EU Delegation as far as needed in the preparation of EU positions.
>
> The monthly Ambassador's luncheons will continue to be hosted by the EU Delegation and the member states on a rotation basis as agreed locally.
>
> Brief summary records will be made by the EU Delegation, with the support of the Belgian Permanent Delegation, for coordination meetings at Ambassadors and Deputies' level. Similar summary records may be made for coordination meetings at committee and working party level, especially when the outcome is to be submitted to the Ambassadors.
>
> **Representation.** Following the entry into force of the Treaty of Lisbon, Statements and Declarations by the European Union are no longer issued by the rotating Presidency, but under the authority of the High Representative.
>
> As a matter of principle the EU Delegation will speak for the EU on areas of exclusive and shared competences, when a common position has been reached. In case the Belgian Presidency is asked to speak on behalf of the European Union, it will do so on behalf of the High Representative.
>
> The EU Delegation will also speak on behalf of the member states on issues of national competence when requested to do so by the member states and upon a clear and agreed mandate given to the EU Delegation by the member states.
>
> Coordination is required, especially when international agreed instruments and recommendations are elaborated.
>
> *Source*: Extracts from *Working arrangements between the EU Delegation and the Belgian Permanent Representation to the OECD*, working document of 1 September 2010.

At the IEA, which is co-located with the OECD, the Commission is again formally an observer, but with de facto full rights to participate as if a member.

Comment: Upgrading the EU's participation from observer to member (without a vote) would not make a significant difference in functional terms, but could be justified as part of a coherent policy to modernise the EU's presence in international organisations. Post-Lisbon arrangements for how the EU coordinates and represents its positions have been worked out in some detail.

6.2.2 Council of Europe, European Convention (and Court) for Human Rights

The EU is observer at the Council of Europe (CoE), while all member states are members. The Commission does not contribute to the CoE budget directly, but is the largest contributor to joint operating programmes with the CoE. Under a MoU of May 2007 the EU and CoE agreed to enhanced cooperation and reinforced political dialogue, which is led by regular twice-yearly so-called Quadripartite meetings, with the EU represented by (so far) the rotating Council Presidency and the Commission, and the CoE by the Chairman of the Committee of Ministers and the Secretary General.

An upgrade of the status of the EU at the CoE from observer to member would reflect the EU's large responsibilities in the area of CoE competences, and the extensive operational cooperation that has developed in recent years. However there is a new and specific trigger point prompting reconsideration of the EU's status there. This is because the Lisbon Treaty has decided that the EU shall accede to the European Convention for Human Rights and Fundamental Freedoms (ECHR) and therefore also become direct stakeholder in the work of the European Court of Human Rights (ECtHR). This will mean that complaints against the EU within the ECtHR can be brought on the same conditions as those applying to complaints brought against member states, and the EU institutions will be liable to appear as respondents in the case of complaints lodged against them. In June 2010, the Commission received the mandate to negotiate an Accession Agreement with the CoE on behalf of the EU Justice Ministers.[36]

---

[36] Council of the European Union, Council Decision authorising the Commission to negotiate the Accession Agreement of the European Union to the European

Negotiations started in July 2010 and are ongoing, and involve many intricate legal issues over the interface between the jurisdictions of the EU and ECtHR, as well as the prospect of EU financial contributions to the costs of the Court. The European Court of Justice (i.e. the EU Court in Luxembourg) will have a continuous agenda of cases that raise issues of the respective competences of the two courts. Both the Committee of Ministers of the CoE and its Parliamentary Assembly (PACE) have responsibilities for the governance of the Convention and the Court, and all CoE member states are represented as members of these bodies.

It is possible that the forthcoming accession to the ECHR will be followed by consideration of other elements that would further deepen EU-CoE relations, for example accession of the EU to other CoE Conventions and expanded joint programmes. If the EU acceded as full member to the Committee of Ministers there would have to be a procedure for determining agenda items for which the member states were competent and therefore vote, and those involving EU competence on which it would vote (see the procedures at the FAO as an example).

Comment: With the EU acceding to the ECHR, on top of the already substantial EU contributions to joint programmes with the CoE, there is a case for reform of the EU's presence in the CoE. Logically this could go as far as the EU acceding to the Committee of Ministers with the HR alongside foreign ministers there, for Members of the European Parliament to accede to the PACE, and for the EU European Council to nominate a judge to the ECHR.

6.2.3 OSCE

So far the EU has been represented by the Commission as observer, with the rotating Council Presidency taking the lead as spokesperson and coordinator of member state positions in Vienna. Apparently the EU Head of delegation has in the first half of 2010 sat next to the rotating Presidency at the table of ambassadors' meetings, but this is a transitional anomaly that will presumably end with that of the rotating Presidency's role.

At the Astana OSCE summit in December 2010, the protocol arrangements for the EU delegation to intervene (at the level of Van Rompuy) were pragmatic, notably by comparison with the unresolved

---

Convention for the Protection of Human Rights and Fundamental Freedoms (ECHR), 10569/10, Brussels, 2 June 2010.

problem at the UNGA. It was decided that the general order of intervention will be determined by the drawing of lots, and that the EU delegation *"may take the floor immediately before or after the participating State holding the EU Presidency without setting a precedent and without altering the existing Rules of Procedure of the OSCE".*[37]

OSCE ministers meet frequently in informal sessions called the 'Corfu Process', which was started to debate the Medvedev proposal for a European Security Treaty. The HR participates there freely given the informality.

There is no formal core group at the OSCE. It has been suggested that the OSCE might create one in the style of the UNSC, with permanent places for major states and the EU. Such a reform seems desirable because of the unwieldy plenary meetings of 56 member states and need for a compact group capable of making decisions in emergencies (e.g. for cases like that of Kyrgyzstan in spring-summer 2010. An executive committee or steering group might consist of the EU, Russia and the US as permanent members, accompanied by the Troika of three rotating presidencies (past, current, next) which would also assure representation of smaller member states especially from non-EU countries. However it is extremely difficult to achieve consensus for formal reforms of this kind. The result is that other less institutionalised arrangements may develop. For example there is the Merkel-Medvedev proposal for a new EU-Russia bilateral security dialogue, involving the HR and Russian foreign ministers, which is currently under discussion. A variant on this could see a trialogue with the US joining in, which would be an interesting way to broaden the Russia-US 'reset'. Such developments would come close to a de facto OSCE steering group.

Comment: While the innovations of the Lisbon Treaty in the foreign and security policy field make it now timely for the EU to be fully represented as member of the OSCE alongside the member states, there are more profound reforms needed for the OSCE to become more effective, including the creation of a restricted steering group or executive committee in which the EU could have a seat, failing which less formal formats may emerge bypassing the OSCE.

---

[37] OSCE, Decision No. 951, Agenda, Organizational Framework, Timetable and other Modalities of the OSCE Summit at Astana on 1 and 2 December 2010.

6.2.4 European Economic Area (EEA)

According to the EEA Agreement, the EU should be represented in the EEA Council by the EU Council and the Commission. In practice, pre-Lisbon, the EU has been represented by a 'troika' of four: the current rotating Council Presidency, the Council Secretariat, the Commission (DG Relex) and the next rotating Presidency. While the EEA Council meetings are supposed to take place at ministerial level, it is rare for more than one principal (typically the Foreign Minister or Economics Minister of the rotating Presidency) to be present, with the others represented by state secretaries, deputy director-generals, etc. Ministerial-level participation is however quite common during the informal political dialogue, which takes place just before the formal meetings of the EEA Council.

At the November 2010 meeting of the EEA Council, the EU representation was led by the rotating Belgian Presidency, accompanied by the Commission. This was in line with the fact that the rotating Presidency continues to chair the EFTA Working Group of the Council, which means the EEA is being assimilated to the internal market affairs of the EU, rather than its external relations. Pre-Lisbon a high official of DG Relex was the lead EU representative, rather than the DGs responsible for internal market or trade.

Comment: Post-Lisbon the EU's representation in the EEA Council has continued to be led by the rotating Council Presidency, implicitly interpreting EEA affairs as internal rather than external business.

6.2.5 EBRD

This is so far a unique case where the EU is a double shareholder (Commission and European Investment Bank) on a par with the member states of the EU and other non-EU states. The Commission and the EIB have Executive Directors, while the smaller member states are organised in constituencies. The EU as a whole has a 64% majority on the board. Steering groups and committees are formed for specialised topics, where the EU will generally be strongly represented. The EU and the member states meet together as a caucus within the EBRD to coordinate and work out common positions.

Comment: The status quo is satisfactory, largely reflecting the fact that the institution is relatively new and so has not inherited older and now politically obsolete structures.

6.2.6 Energy Charter Treaty

This treaty, signed in 1994, was intended to bind the whole of the former Soviet Union, and especially Russia, into a legally binding regulatory space for the energy sector. The contracting parties included the EU itself and the whole of Europe plus Mongolia, with the US, Canada, and many oil-producing countries as observers. However its attempt to agree a legally binding 'transit protocol' failed to win the acceptance of Russia, and in 2009 Russia announced its withdrawal from the treaty as a whole. Institutionally the EU is a full party together with all member states, with the Commission generally representing the EU position in restricted preparatory meetings and plenary sessions.

Comment: Institutionally the status quo is satisfactory, again because of its recent origins, but the organisation fails to meet its major objectives, given Russia's withdrawal.

6.2.7 Energy Community Treaty (for South-East Europe)

Not to be confused with the Energy Charter Treaty, this Energy Community Treaty entered into force in July 2006 and initially brought together the EC, and since Lisbon the EU, and seven Balkan non-member states (including UNMIK for Kosovo). Its function is to extend the EU's core energy *acquis* to these non-member states and thus widen the EU's internal energy market. In December 2009 Moldova and Ukraine became further full contracting parties. There is a secretariat in Vienna, separate from the Commission. At meetings of the governing bodies the Commission alone speaks, while the member states are invited to participate in discussion (about 13 member states make use of this provision).

Comment: Institutionally the status quo is satisfactory, again because of its recent origins, and the organisation progresses with more a compact geographical coverage than the Energy Charter.

6.2.8 NATO

Official relations between the EU and NATO were launched in 2001 in an exchange of letters between the NATO Secretary General and the EU Presidency. This has subsequently developed into what is officially described as a 'strategic partnership'. There are regular meetings at all levels: foreign ministers, ambassadors, military representatives and defence advisers, and between the NATO International Staff and the EU Council Secretariat and Military Staff. The EU HR is invited to all NATO ministerial meetings as participant with speaking rights; and the NATO Secretary General is invited to EU foreign and defence ministers' meetings selectively, given their frequency, for agenda items of common interests. The NATO Secretary General and EU HR meet regularly, about once a month, accompanied by senior military staff. Permanent military liaison arrangements have been established: a NATO Permanent Liaison Team has been located with the EU Military Staff since 2005, and an EU Cell was set up at the NATO strategic command centre at SHAPE in 2006. A joint NATO-EU Declaration on the EU's European Security and Defence Policy of 2002 reaffirmed the EU's assured access to NATO's planning capabilities and the principles of mutual consultation with due regard to the decision-making autonomy of both parties.

The ambassadors of NATO in the North Atlantic Council (NAC) and of the EU in the Political and Security Committee (PSC) have occasional joint meetings, which are said to be rather dull affairs, attributable perhaps to the unwieldy format of over 50 ambassadors, or possibly because of the limited agendas (due at least in part to the Turkey-Cyprus hiatus – see further below).

There is one pragmatic element of institutional fusion, in that many EU member states 'double-hat' their members of the EU and NATO Military Committees – i.e. the same senior military office serves both positions at the same time – which assures mutual transparency and information for operations such as the Somalia anti-piracy missions where both EU and NATO are active.

Operational arrangements were deepened under the so-called 'Berlin-plus' agreement of 2003, which provides for NATO-EU cooperation in crisis management operations, including support by NATO for EU-led operations and notably through access to NATO HQ facilities. These arrangements were first used in the cases of Macedonia and Bosnia where EU forces took over from NATO in 2003 and 2004 respectively. However the formal use of Berlin-plus arrangements seems limited now to Bosnia. The EU and NATO are also now working alongside each other in Kosovo, Afghanistan (where the EU runs rule of law missions alongside NATO's military presence) and in anti-piracy operations in Somalia; but these are not framed within Berlin-plus (again due to the Turkey-Cyprus hiatus).

There are some particular blockages to this cooperation due to the hiatus between Turkey and the EU, with Cyprus as a complicating factor also. Turkey has objected to the effective downgrading of its status with the winding up of the WEU (to be completed legally by 2011) in which it was a virtually full participant, and the transfer of its functions to the EU, where its status is more restricted. In consequence Turkey blocks various cooperative actions between NATO and the EU, for example the request by the EU that NATO extend protection in Afghanistan to EU police personnel if need be. Given that Turkey has blocked this request, the EU must negotiate agreements bilaterally with NATO member states. It is generally agreed that ways must be found to lift this hiatus, but this has not yet been done. An example of a constructive initiative would be for the EU to invite Turkey to become formally associated with, or member of, the European Defence Agency. Then the absurd stand-off between Turkey and the EU in relation to NATO might be moderated.

While there have been some useful developments in EU-NATO institutional relations, the operational content of the relationship is still limited. NATO's Secretary General is speaking out in favour of "a true strategic partnership between NATO and the European Union. ...NATO and the EU are two of the world's most important institutions. They share 21 members. They have complementary skills. And no other strategic partnership would offer so many benefits -- both operationally and financially."[38] Concretely there are issues of coherence and coordination over the assignment of forces to NATO and the EU respectively, which exemplify the need for closer cooperation. There are overlapping assignments of force numbers to the EU's 'Headline Goals' and NATO's 'Defence Planning', since the same troops can in theory appear under both headings. On the other hand, the EU Battle Groups and NATO Response Force have to be separately identified contingents.

Apart from the Turkey-related problems, this sounds like it has the potential to become a quite rich relationship, but informal comments by officials suggest a less positive story, with commonplace remarks about "the two organisations living on different planets", albeit about 5 km away

---

[38] Anders Fogh Rasmussen, "Security in an Era of Budgetary Scarcity", keynote speech at conference on NATO's European Dimension, organised by the Security and Defence Agenda and the Konrad Adenauer Stiftung, Brussels, 21 June 2010.

from each other. At the 18-19 November 2010 NATO summit in Lisbon, President Van Rompuy spoke on behalf of the EU at a working dinner of NATO leaders, reportedly saying that "the ability of our two organisations to shape our future security would be enormous if they worked together. It is time to break down the remaining walls between us". Given that informal relationships in the small town of Brussels do not seem to develop easily, there is a case for making some more formal arrangements. The easiest to initiate would be for NATO and the EU to swap mutual observer relationships at the level of ambassadors in NATO's North Atlantic Council (NAC) and the EU's Political and Security Committee (PSC).

Comment: A principal issue for the EU and its member states is whether they will want at some stage to form an 'EU caucus' within NATO and so present more structured common positions on key policy issues. The US has so far been unenthusiastic about this, but this might change if the EU side shaped up more clearly. Much less difficult for the short run, the EU might have a permanent observer at the ambassador level (for example the EU PSC chairperson, ex-officio) on the North Atlantic Council, and this could be reciprocated with a NATO observer at the PSC.

6.3   Semi-institutionalised summitry and diplomacy

6.3.1   G7/8/20

G7. With the admission of Russia to the G8, the G7 has become no more than an economic forum, in which the EU is represented by the President of the European Central Bank (EU delegation=1 person). France, Germany, Italy and the United Kingdom are represented by their Finance Ministers and Central Bank Governors. The European Commission and the President of the eurozone (since its creation) are only occasionally invited to attend G7 meetings. G7 meetings are prepared on the EU side by the Eurogroup Working Group for matters related to eurozone competences, and the Economic and Financial Committee preparing other matters.

G8. The EU is represented by the Presidents of the European Council and Commission at Summit level (EU delegation=2 people), alongside France, Germany, Italy and the UK. With the Lisbon Treaty now in force, Barroso and Van Rompuy both sit at the table, but only one speaks in the name of the EU depending on the issue. The EU sherpa is the sherpa of the President of the European Council, whereas the sous-sherpa is the sherpa of the President of the Commission.

Opinions apparently differ on whether the EU is a real 'member' of the G8 or not (for instance, the EU is sometimes mentioned on the G8 website as a member, sometimes not), but in practice the EU enjoys the same 'rights' as any other G8 member in being invited to all meetings with the right to speak, but not the right to host or chair a summit. There is no EU coordination before G8 meetings. Non-G8 EU countries are not involved in the G8 process and are only kept informed. The Commission and the EU President receive no specific mandates to speak at the G8 on behalf of the EU, which means that they are free to speak about everything but cannot commit to anything.

G20. In the original G20, the EU was represented by the President of the European Central Bank plus the ECOFIN Presidency (the President of the Eurogroup was not present), and the Commission only participated at a technical level in the delegation. France, Germany, Italy and the UK are represented by their Finance Ministers and Central Bank Governors.

In the 'new' summit-level G20, established November 2008, member states are represented by their Heads of State and Government, while the EU is represented by both the European Council and Commission Presidents. Van Rompuy speaks on foreign policy and security matters, whereas Barroso speaks on areas of exclusive EU competence. In areas of shared competence, they decide on a case-by-case basis who will speak in the name of the EU. The official Canadian G20 Presidency website for the June 2010 meeting stated that the G20 consists of 19 states with the EU as 20th full participant,[39] and this has been repeated on the Korean official website too. Other participants, described in some documents as 'Outreach Participants',[40] include the Netherlands and Spain, who have been invited to four successive summits.

As the Lisbon Treaty does not mention the G7/8/20, there is no explicit ruling on how the EU should be represented. At the November 2010 summit in Seoul, the EU was represented by Van Rompuy and

---

[39] Five seats for the EU (France, Germany, Italy, UK, EU), 3 seats for Latin America (Argentina, Brazil, Mexico), 5 seats for Asia (China, India, Indonesia, Japan, Korea), 1 from Africa (South Africa), 1 from the Arab world (Saudi Arabia), and Australia, Canada, Russia, Turkey and US.

[40] The Netherlands, Spain, Ethiopia, Malawi and Vietnam, and leadership of the Financial Stability Board, ILO, IMF, OECD, UN, World Bank and WTO.

Barroso, without the Belgian rotating Council Presidency, although Belgium was still represented at the G20 finance ministers meeting in October 2010. At ministerial level, the EU is thus represented by the Commission, the ECB and the rotating Presidency (EU delegation at ministerial level = 3 people).

As opposed to the G8, the EU makes more effort to coordinate its position ahead of the G20 summits, providing mandates for its representatives to negotiate in the name of the EU on selected issues. The Sherpa of the EU is the Sherpa of the Commission, whereas the sous-sherpa is the Sherpa of the President (in symmetry with G8: i.e. G8 is primarily political, hence predominance of the Council, while the G20 is primarily economic and financial, hence predominance of the Commission).

The representation of the EU by two Presidents at the G20 summit level will be seen increasingly as an anomaly. An ad hoc solution would be for the two Presidents to reach an understanding for one or the other but not both to represent the EU on different occasions. In the long-run, maybe around 2020, there may build up arguments in favour of rationalising the EU's leadership by combining the posts of Commission and European Council Presidents in one person. While this would be a major institutional reform that would only happen for profound political reasons going beyond matters of external representation, it should be noted that there is nothing in the Lisbon Treaty to prevent the European Council from taking such a decision without a need for treaty change.

At the meetings of the G20 finance ministers, the Council has made more detailed arrangements, after considering legal opinions prepared by the legal services of the Council[41] and Commission as to whether arrangements should be modified post-Lisbon. The Council decided to continue with the status quo, with the EU to be represented by the Commission, European Central Bank and the rotating Council Presidency. In particular France in its capacity as incoming G20 Presidency is inviting Hungary to the meetings in the first half of 2010. The justification for inviting the rotating Council Presidency merits explanation, since this position is not mentioned in the Lisbon Treaty, where Article 17.1 TEU in

---

[41] Opinion of the Legal Service of the Council of the European Union, "The representation of the Union and its member States at the Group of Twenty", 16451/10, 17 November 2010.

particular only mentions the Commission and High Representative. However this article allows for exceptions provided elsewhere in the Treaties, as notably in Article 138 (TFEU), which deals with the representation of the eurozone in international meetings. In addition for areas where the member states are competent the Council may designate whomsoever it wishes to represent them, with the rotating Council Presidency one such possibility.

Comment: Post-Lisbon, the situation at G8/20 summit level meetings may be considered satisfactory in a narrow sense for the EU institutions, since both Van Rompuy and Barroso are admitted. However for the future it is anomalous for the EU to have these two seats on top of four member states while the US and others have only one head of state or government. The EU should find one method or another of cutting its representation to one President. For G20 finance ministers meetings the EU representation will still include the rotating Council Presidency.

6.3.2 Bilateral summits (strategic partnership cases)

The EU-Russia summit of June 2010 made a clean break from pre- to post-Lisbon regimes. The EU was represented there by Van Rompuy and Barroso, with Ashton and the Trade Commissioner, while the rotating Council Presidency was no longer present. The complete set of strategic partnership summits consists of the US, Canada, Japan, Russia, China, India, Japan, Brazil and India, with regular summits also with Pakistan and Ukraine, and with the possible addition of South Korea also mooted.

It is notable that the Spanish rotating Presidency tried to host a US summit in the first half of 2010, which Obama declined to attend, citing other preoccupations. Given the confusion at that time over the transition to the post-Lisbon model, the US position was understandable.

Comment: The post-Lisbon representation of the EU sees the disappearance of the rotating Council Presidency, but given the large number of bilateral summits, it remains to be seen whether the EU representation will always be as in the Russia example cited. To always have Van Rompuy and Barroso present, although in accordance with the Lisbon Treaty, seems excessive when Russia is represented by Medvedev without Putin.

6.3.3 European neighbourhood and other multilateral regional processes

European Neighbourhood Policy (ENP). This policy has developed since 2003 primarily on the basis of bilateral actions plans negotiated between the

Commission and the six Eastern neighbours and ten Southern Mediterranean neighbours. This activity overlaps with the functioning of the pre-existing Partnership and Cooperation Agreements in the East, and Barcelona Process Association Agreements to the South; to which may be added now new Association Agreements that begin to be negotiated with the Eastern neighbours. The system is further complicated by the Union for the Mediterranean and Eastern Partnership initiatives, to the point that it is best now to discuss East and South separately.

Barcelona Process and Union for the Mediterranean. The addition of the Union for the Mediterranean (UfM) to the Barcelona Process and ENP, upon the initiative of President Sarkozy in 2008, led to a convoluted superimposition of initiatives. Originally an attempt to overarch the Barcelona Process by a new Union that would bring together just the littoral states of the Mediterranean and thus exclude Northern Europe, Sarkozy was forced to backtrack by Chancellor Merkel. When the project eventually took shape, it was endowed with a double presidency, initially France and Egypt. The South-Med presidency was set for a two-year period, but the North-Med presidency was given no clear time limit, in part because of the complications it would cause in relation to the innovations of the Lisbon Treaty, whose outcome was then in 2008 still uncertain. Sarkozy still remains UfM President after two years, with 2010 witnessing institutional confusion on an even grander scale. The Spanish rotating Presidency of the first half of 2010 proposed a UfM summit for June 2010 in Barcelona. Before the EU had time to work out the distribution of roles for this event as between the four presidents who could be involved – Sarkozy, Zapatero, Barroso and Van Rompuy – it was postponed until November because of political frictions with the South Med states over the Middle East. The November conference was also postponed. For the future the leadership of the UfM/Barcelona process might best be regularised, entrusting the EU chairmanship to Van Rompuy and HR Ashton according to the level of the meetings. The UfM has also been endowed with its own secretariat in Barcelona, with complex political bargaining having gone into the allocation of posts, leading to a Jordanian diplomat appointed Secretary General. Continuing work of the ENP in the South, and Cooperation Council meetings under the Association Agreements, will be done by the HR/EEAS, without the rotating Council Presidency.

Comment: While the initial conception of the UfM would have meant disruption of the EU's external policies on a grand scale, this has been largely averted. Regularisation of the Presidency on the EU side remains to be sorted out, while the two successive postponements of the UfM summit makes for unfavourable comparisons with the Eastern Partnership.

ENP/Eastern Partnership. The Eastern Partnership (EaP) was initiated in 2009 following a Polish-Swedish proposal with a view to boosting the Eastern branch of the ENP. In practice the EaP has become a regional-multilateral supplement to the essentially bilateral workings of the ENP. Bilateral Cooperation Council meetings with the Eastern partner states will now be led on the EU side by the HR/EEAS, and negotiations of new Association Agreements will be led by the HR/EEAS in teamwork with relevant Commission DGs. The multilateral ministerial meetings of the Eastern Partnership will be done by the HR together with the responsible Commissioner. The rotating Presidency was in principle to be no longer active in the EaP, but the forthcoming Council Presidencies for 2011, successively Hungary and Poland, have indicated that they are highly interested, with Hungary to host a summit meeting in May 2011.

Comment: This was set to become a normal model case, post-Lisbon, but the rotating Council Presidencies of 2011 seek to make a comeback.

Northern Dimension. This multilateral initiative was launched by Finland in 1998 and brought together Russia, Norway and Iceland with the EU27 in an effort to develop good regional cooperation with North-West Russia. The first years of the Northern Dimension saw clumsy ministerial meetings with all member states, many of whom had little interest in the body. In the second and current period, starting in 2007, the Northern Dimension project has been reshaped with just four 'members' – EU, Norway, Iceland and Russia – with the EU to be represented now at ministerial level by the HR or a deputy. But this representation is supplemented by a so-called 'Open Troika', where interested member states can participate.[42]

Comment: The model for the Northern Dimension has developed in an interesting way, with the Nordic states taking the lead in rationalising its institutional features in a more efficient manner, cutting down on excessive participation of member states.

---

[42] For a detailed account, see P. Aalto et al. (eds), *The New Northern Dimension of the European Neighbourhood*, CEPS Paperback, CEPS, 2008.

Asia-Europe Meeting (ASEM). Officially established in 1996, the first ASEM summit took place in Bangkok as an interregional forum consisting of the European Commission, the EU member states, the 13 members of the ASEAN Plus Three (China, Japan, Korea) regional grouping, and, as of 2008, India, Mongolia, and Pakistan. By the 2010 meeting the participation has been further expanded to include Pakistan, India, Russia, Australia and New Zealand, making a total of 48. All parties are in principle present at the level of heads of state for the ASEM Summit, which is organised every other year (with other meetings on the margins, as well as ahead of the Summit) and hosted alternatively by the EU and Asia. There is no common EU position prepared for these meetings, although there are some consultations on the agenda, notably through the Asia-Oceania Working Party (COASI) in the Council. With 48 parties present, these are huge numbers of people present at what is essentially a quite loose conference process. Until 2010, the EU was represented by the Commission as full member (as was also the Secretariat of ASEAN). Belgium as rotating Council Presidency was in charge of organising the 2010 Summit on 3-4 October, but agreed that Herman Van Rompuy would chair the meeting, flanked by President Barroso and the Belgian Prime Minister. These new arrangements have triggered some concern from the Asian side that this might lead to lowering the level of member state representation ("Europe does not equal the EU"), and that therefore this EU chairmanship should be no precedent for future ASEM summits.

The EU has not been participating in the East Asia summit process, which includes India, China, Japan, Korea, the Asian states and Australia, as well as Russia and the US. There have been hesitations over the EU's possible participation, initially on the EU side and subsequently on the side of ASEAN over whether the EU as a non-state party could join in.

Comment: The new post-Lisbon changes in the representation of the EU create some concerns with the Asian partners in relation to the ASEM process, while the EU has been so far absent from the East Asia summit process.

Latin America and Caribbean. The 6th EU-LAC Summit of Heads of State and Government took place in Madrid on 18 May 2010. In its margins, no less than six other bilateral mini-Summits were held with specific LAC countries and sub-regions,[43] which seems to have been a suitably economical use of time. The EU was represented at all these events by Van Rompuy, Barroso and (for the rotating Council Presidency) Zapatero. The rotating Presidency will no longer appear at these events in future.

Comment: The post-Lisbon rules were not applied by the Spanish rotating Presidency in the first half of 2010, but should prevail in future.

African Union. The 3rd EU-Africa Summit of Heads of State and Government took place in Libya in November 2010. The first Summit was held in Cairo in 2000 and the second Summit in 2007 under the Portuguese rotating Presidency. This second Summit led to the adoption of the Africa-EU Strategic Partnership which sets the main framework for the relationship and plans among other things a Summit every three years. During Summits, in addition to the Heads of State and Government of African and European member states, the EU has so far been represented by the rotating Presidency, the President of the Commission and the Secretary General/High Representative. Switching to the post-Lisbon rules, in Libya the EU was represented by Van Rompuy, Barroso and Commissioner Piebalgs. Aside from the summits, there are other established dialogues at ministerial and at parliamentary level.

Comment: The EU was represented at the November 2010 summit by the normal post-Lisbon model – with both Van Rompuy and Barroso in the lead.

6.3.4 Conflict prevention/resolution

Solana built up a set of 11 Special Representatives (SRs) for the conflict zones of the Balkans, Caucasus, Central Asia, Middle East, Afghanistan and Africa. The role of the SRs is due to be revised. Some may be merged and double-hatted with the Heads of Delegations as already is the case in Macedonia and Afghanistan. Others such as for Central Asia seem likely to be maintained.

Israel-Palestine. Since 2002 the Quartet has assembled the US, the EU, Russia and the UN. The EU has so far been represented by a Special Representative and the Commission. A decade ago, the Special Representative was Ambassador Miguel Angel Moratinos, until recently

---

[43] EU–Andean Community (CAN), Central America Summit, Caribbean Forum (CARIFORUM), EU-Chile Summit, EU-Mexico Summit and EU-Mercosur.

foreign minister of Spain, but the post is currently held by a lower-profile diplomat. The post should be filled by someone with high political stature.

Bosnia. The quasi-protectorate regime under the Dayton Agreement and with the 'Bonn powers' has been led at the international level by the Peace Implementation Council (PIC), which brings together on the EU side most but not all member states as members or observers with the Commission and Council rotating Presidency, alongside the US, Russia, Turkey, Canada, etc. The Office of the High Representative (OHR), vested with the Bonn powers, is double-hatted with the EU Special Representative. The next step that is generally considered desirable, but subject to much political debate over the conditions for doing this, would be for the OHR to be scrapped, or at least de-linked from the EUSR, who might then be double-hatted with the EU Head of Delegation in Sarajevo.

Kosovo. The EU has had an SR in Kosovo since 2007. From 2008, when Kosovo declared independence, this position has been double-hatted with that of International Civil Representative (ICO). In addition Kosovo sees the largest EU external operational mission, with the EULEX rule of law staffed with a target of 3,200 staff, of which 1,950 are Europeans.

Macedonia. The conflict prevention mission has led to the Special Representative being double-hatted with the Head of Delegation in Skopje.

South Caucasus. The region has three unresolved conflicts: Nagorno-Karabakh, Abkhazia and South Ossetia. However responsibility for pursuing resolution of the conflicts is diffused. For Nagorno-Karabakh, the search for a settlement between Armenia and Azerbaijan is headed since 1992 by the OSCE-sponsored 'Minsk Group', effectively run by its three co-chairs from Russia, the US and France (representing France, not the EU). For Georgia and its conflict with the secessionist provinces Abkhazia and South Ossetia, the lead group until the August 2008 war was the UN-sponsored 'Friends of the Secretary General' group for Georgia, including France, Germany, the UK, Russia and the US (without EU representation). However after the August 2008 war, the centre of activity has been in the 'Geneva Process' co-chaired by the OSCE, the UN and the EU. The EU is here represented by Ambassador Pierre Morel, who is also Special Representative for Central Asia, and was brought in by President Sarkozy in implementation of the French/EU 6 point peace plan that ended the war. The EU has since 2003 had a Special Representative for the region as a whole, with the post held since 2006 by a Swedish diplomat, but his position sits uneasily alongside the other special representatives mentioned. This situation should be rationalised, with a single EU SR for the whole of the Caucasus and all of the conflicts.

Moldova-Transnistria. Since 2005 the EU, together with the US, joined as observers a pre-existing mediation process now called '5+2' mediation format, bringing together Russia-Ukraine-Romania-US-EU together with the Republic of Moldova and the Transnistria. Activation of this mediation mechanism has since 2006 been blocked by Russia, but may be re-activated in the foreseeable future. There has been an EUSR responsible for Moldova since 2005. For the future this position could be combined with that of an enhanced EU Delegation in Chisinau. Another formula could combine the position with a Caucasus EUSR, thus having the same person to deal with all of the unresolved conflicts of the former Soviet area.

Central Asia. This post of Special Representative was created in 2005 and was enhanced in importance with the adoption by the EU in 2007 of its Central Asia Strategy. The special justification of this position lies in the fact that the EU has so far been very incompletely represented by Delegations in the region, and so the Special Representative functions as a roving ambassador for the EU.[44]

Afghanistan. Since January 2010 of there is a double-hatted SR and Head of Delegation in Kabul.

Comment: With the EEAS coming into service, the role of the SR is being reviewed, without decisions yet known. This review is indeed pertinent. The upgrading of EU Delegations may facilitate in some cases further double-hatting of the SR with the Heads of Delegation. On the other hand, double-hatting of SRs with international roles (as in Bosnia, Kosovo) should be temporary only, since it risks creating conflicts of interest.

---

[44] For a detailed review see M. Emerson et al., *Into EurAsia – Monitoring the EU's Central Asia Strategy*, CEPS Paperback, CEPS, Brussels, 2010.

Glossary

ASEM	Asia-Europe Meetings
BIS	Bank for International Settlements
DG	Directorate General
EaP	Eastern Partnership
ECHR	European Convention for Human Rights
ECtHR	European Court for Human Rights
EBRD	European Bank for Reconstruction and Development
EEA	European Economic Area
EEAS	European External Action Service
ENP	European Neighbourhood Policy
EUSR	EU Special Representative
FAO	Food and Agriculture Organization
HR	High Representative of the Union for Foreign Affairs and Security Policy and Vice-President of the Commission
ICAO	International Civil Aviation Organization
ICC	International Criminal Court
ICJ	International Court of Justice
ICO	International Civil Representative (Kosovo)
IEA	International Energy Agency
IFAD	International Fund for Agricultural Development
IFI	International Financial Institutions
ILO	International Labour Organization
IMF	International Monetary Fund
IMO	International Maritime Organization
IOM	International Organization for Migration
ITU	International Telecommunications Union
LAC	Latin American and Caribbean
MS	Member state(s) of the EU

NATO	North Atlantic treaty Organization
OECD	Organisation for Economic Cooperation and Development
OHCHR	Office of the UN High Commissioner for Human Rights
OHR	Office of the High Representative (Bosnia)
OSCE	Organisation for Security and Cooperation in Europe
PIC	Peace Implementation Council (Bosnia)
TEU	Treaty on European Union
TFEU	Treaty on the Functioning of the European Union
UfM	Union for the Mediterranean
UNCTAD	UN Conference on Trade and Development
UNDP	UN Development Programme
UNEP	UN Environment Programme
UNFCCC	UN Framework Convention on Climate Change
UNHCR	UN High Commission for Refugees
UNGA	UN General Assembly
UNSC	UN Security Council
UPU	Universal Postal Union
WCO	World Customs Organization
WFP	World Food Programme
WHO	World Health Organization
WIPO	World Intellectual Property Organization
WTO	World Trade Organization

ANNEXES

Annex A. Overview of EU Participation in the UN System

UNGA　　General Assembly　　Observer

UNGA dependent programmes and funds

UNCTAD (trade/develop.)	Observer
ENEP (environment)	Observer
UNICEF (children)	Observer
UNDP (development)	Observer
UNFPA (population)	Observer
UNHCR (refugees)	Observer, request for full participant
UNRWA (refugees)	Observer
UNCITRAL (trade law)	Observer

ECOSOC　　　　　　　　　Observer

ECOSOC Commissions

CHR (human rights)	Observer
CND (narcotics)	Observer
CCPCJ (crime)	Observer
CSD (sustain. develop.)	Full participant
CSW (women)	Observer
CPD (population/develop.)	Observer
CSOD (social develop.)	Observer
Statistical Commission	Observer

ECOSOC Regional Commissions

ECA (Africa)	Observer subject to invitation
ECE (Europe)	Observer subject to invitation
ECLAC (Lat Amer/Carib)	Observer subject to invitation

118 | ANNEXES

ESCAP (Asia/Pac) — Observer subject to invitation
ESCWA (West Asia) — Observer subject to invitation
UNFF (forests) — Observer

UN specialised agencies
ILO — Observer
FAO — Member
UNESCO — Observer
WHO — Observer
ICAO civil aviation — Observer subject to invitation
IMO — Permanent observer
WIPO — Observer, full participant in some committees
IFAO — Observer in Gov, Council but not Ex. Com.
IBRD — none
IDA — none
IFC — none
MIGA — none
IMF — ECB invited to Ex. Board selectively
IAEA — Observer
Codex Alimentarius — Member
ISA (seabed authority) — Member

UN Conferences
UNCED (sustainable dev.) — Full participant
WSSD (sustainable dev.) — Full participant
Small islands, 1994 — Observer
Small islands, 2005 — Full participant
UNCTAD (trade/dev.) — Observer
UNCLDC (least developed) — Full participant
CFD (financing) — Full participant
WCDR (disaster reduction) — Observer, de facto full participant
WCHR (human rights) — Observer

WCRRDX (xenophobia)	Full participant
WCW (women)	Full participant
UNHS (habitats)	Observer
ICPD (population/dev)	Full participant
WCMRY (youth)	Observer subject to invitation
WSSD (social develop.)	Full participant
WAA (ageing)	Observer
WFS (food)	Member
UNCICC (criminal court)	Observer
UNCPCTO (crime)	Observer
UNCTOC (crime)	Observer
UNCITSALW (small arms)	Full participant
NPT (nuclear non-prolif.)	Observer agency status
UNCLOS (fish stocks)	Member
CCCD (desertification)	Member
UNCCC (climate change)	Member
UNISPACE (outer space)	Observer
WSIS (information soc.)	Full participant

UN Conventions

UNFSA (fish stocks)	Full member
UNCCC (climate change)	Full member
UNCND (narcotics)	Full member
UNCTOC (crime)	Full member
UN LINER (conferences)	Full member
UNCLOS (law of sea)	Full member
UNCC (corruption)	Full member
UNCCD (desertification)	Full member

Annex B. International Organisations and Conventions in which the EU Participates fully by virtue of a Regional Economic Integration Organisation (REIO) or Regional Integration Organisation (RIO) clause

Industrial Technical

Regulations for wheeled vehicles 1997, 2000
European pharmacopeia (Council of Europe), 1994
Maintenance operations, 2009
International nickel study group, 1991
International tin study group, 1991

Agriculture & Food

Common fund for commodities, 1990
Jute Study Group, 2002
FAO, 1991
Food aid convention, 1999
Grains trade convention, 1996
Olive oil & table olives agreement, 2005
International cocoa agreement, 2001
International coffee agreement, 2001, 2007
International sugar agreement, 1992
International tropical timber agreement, 2007
WHO tobacco control convention, 2004

Fisheries

Fisheries Commission for Mediterranean, 1998
Indian Ocean Tuna Commission, 1995
Highly migratory fish stocks, 1998
Small cetaceans in Baltic & North Seas, 1945
Fishing vessels on high seas, 1996
Salmon in North Atlantic (NASCO), 1982
Inter-American tropical tuna, 2005

Northeast Atlantic fisheries (NEAFC), 1981
Migratory fish in west &central Pacific, 2005
Conservation Atlantic tuna (ICCAT), 1986
South Indian Ocean fisheries, 2006

Environment
African-Eurasian migratory waterbirds, 2006
Dolphin Conservation Programme, 1999
Convention Law of the Sea (UNCLOS) , 1994, 1998
Transboundary hazardous waste, Basle,1993
Biosafety, biological diversity, Cartagena, 2002
Marine environment north-east Atlantic, 1998
Protection against Mediterrannean pollution, Barcelona, 1997
Justice in environmental matters, 2005
Convention on biological diversity, 1993
Protection of river Danube, 1997
Long range trans-boundary air pollution, 1981
Desertification in Africa, 1998
Antarctic marine living resources (CCAMLR), 1981
Migratory wild animals (Bonn), 1982
Transboundary watercourses and lakes, 1995
Marine environment of Baltic Sea (Helsinki), 1994
UN Convention on Climate Change, 1994
Kyoto Protocol, 2002
Heavy metals and transboundary air pollution, 2001
Pollutant release & transfer registers, 2006
Nitrogen oxides, transboundary air pollution, 1993
Monitoring transmission of air pollutants, 1986
Reduction of sulphur emissions, 1998
Hazardous chemicals in international trade, 2003
Persistent organic pollutants (Stockholm), 2006
Protection of ozone layer, 1988

Transport & customs
Rules of international air carriage, 2001
Containers in international transport, 1995
Mobile equipment on aircraft, 2009
Temporary import of comm. road vehicles, 1994
Temporary import of private road vehicles, 1994
Harmonisation frontier control of goods, 1984

Energy
Energy Charter Treaty, 1994
Energy Charter – environmental aspects, 1994
Radioactive waste management, 2005

Justice and home affairs
Choice of court agreement, 2009
Temporary admission convention (Istanbul), 1993
Trafficking of firearms, ammunition 2100
Smuggling of migrants, 2006
Trafficking of women & children, 2006
UN Convention against corruption, 2008

Social policy
Rights of person with disabilities, 2010

Culture
Protection diversity of cultural expressions, 2006

Annex C. Overview of EU Participation in International Maritime Organizations

Contracting party / full member (EC only)
International Commission for the Conservation of Atlantic Tunas (ICCAT)
Indian Ocean Tuna Commission (IOTC)
Western and Central Pacific Fisheries Commission (WCPFC)
South East Atlantic Fisheries Organization (SEAFO)
Northwest Atlantic Fisheries Organization (NAFO)
North Atlantic Salmon Conservation Organization (NASCO)
North East Atlantic Fisheries Commission (NEAFC)

Contracting party / full member (EC + member states)
UN Convention on the Law of the Sea (UNCLOS)
Convention on Environmental Impact Assessment in a Transboundary Context (EIA)
Convention for the Protection of the Marine Environment of the North-East Atlantic (OSPAR)
Helsinki Commission for the Protection of the Marine Environment of the Baltic Sea Area (HELCOM)
Barcelona Convention for the Protection of the Marine Environment (BARCOM)
UN Food and Agriculture Organization (FAO)
United Nations Agreement on Straddling Fish Stocks and Highly Migratory Fish Stocks (UNFSA)
General Fisheries Commission for the Mediterranean (GFCM)
International Baltic Sea Fishery Commission (IBSFC)
Commission for the Conservation of Antarctic Marine Living Resources (CCAMLR)
Convention on the Conservation of Migratory Species of Wild Animals (CMS)
Convention on Biological Diversity (CBD)

Agreement on the International Dolphin Conservation Programme (AIDCP)

Basel Convention on the Control of Transboundary Movements of Hazardous Wastes and their Disposal

Rotterdam Convention on ... Certain Hazardous Chemicals and Pesticides in International Trade

Bonn Agreement on Action Plan to combat illegal and accidental pollution of the Greater North Sea

Convention on Transboundary Effects of Industrial Accidents (TBEIA)

UN Convention of Illicit Traffic Narcotic Drugs

UN Convention on Transnational Organized Crime

Full participant

United Nations Commission on Sustainable Development (CSD)

Observer status for European Commission

Convention on Wetlands of International Importance especially as Waterfowl Habitat (RAMSAR)

Cartagena Convention for the Protection and Development of the Marine Environment in the Wider Caribbean Region

United Nations Environment Programme (UNEP)

Bucharest Convention on the Protection of the Black Sea Against Pollution

Commission for the Conservation of Southern Bluefin Tuna (CCSBT82)

International Whaling Commission (IWC)

Convention on International Trade in Endangered Species of Wild Fauna and Flora (CITES)

Inter-American Tropical Tuna Commission (IATTC830

International Maritime Organization (IMO)

Source: Derived from Wouters, op. cit.

I

Annex D. Voting Weights on the Board of the IMF

EU	% on total	Non-EU	% on total
Germany	5.87	United States	16.74
United Kingdom	4.85	Japan	6.01
France	4.85	China	3.65
Italy	3.19	Canada	2.88
Netherlands	2.34	Russia	2.69
Belgium	2.08	India	1.88
Spain	1.38	Switzerland	1.57
Sweden	1.09	Australia	1.47
Austria	0.85	Mexico	1.43
Denmark	0.75	Brazil	1.38
Poland	0.63	Korea	1.33
Finland	0.58	Argentina	0.96
Hungary	0.48	Indonesia	0.95
Romania	0.48	South Africa	0.85
Portugal	0.40	Nigeria	0.80
Ireland	0.39	Norway	0.76
Greece	0.38	Iran	0.69
Czech Republic	0.38	Malaysia	0.68
Bulgaria	0.30	Turkey	0.55
Slovak Republic	0.17	Libya	0.52
Luxembourg	0.14	Thailand	0.50
Slovenia	0.12	Pakistan	0.48
Lithuania	0.08	Egypt	0.44
Latvia	0.07	Singapore	0.40
Cyprus	0.07		
Malta	0.06		
Estonia	0.04		
Eurozone 16	22.87		
Total EU27	32.02	**Total non-EU**	67.98

Annex E. Voting Weights on the Board of the World Bank, before and after 2010 Reform

EU	% before reform	% after reform	Non-EU	% before reform	% after reform
Germany	4.48	4.00	United States	16.36	15.85
France	4.30	3.75	Japan	7.85	6.84
United Kingdom	4.30	3.75	Canada	2.78	2.43
Italy	2.78	2.64	China	2.78	4.42
Netherlands	2.21	1.92	India	2.78	2.91
Belgium	1.80	1.57	Russian Federation	2.78	2.77
Spain	1.74	1.85	Saudi Arabia	2.78	2.77
Sweden	0.94	0.85	Brazil	2.07	2.24
Denmark	0.85	0.76	Switzerland	1.66	1.46
Austria	0.70	0.63	Australia	1.52	1.33
Poland	0.69	0.73	Iran	1.48	1.47
Finland	0.54	0.50	Venezuela	1.27	1.11
Hungary	0.51	0.47	Mexico	1.18	1.68
Czech Republic	0.40	0.36	Argentina	1.12	1.12
Portugal	0.35	0.34	Korea	0.99	1.57
Bulgaria	0.34	0.30	Indonesia	0.94	0.98
Ireland	0.34	0.35	South Africa	0.85	0.76
Romania	0.26	0.31	Kuwait	0.83	0.83
Slovak Republic	0.21	0.20	Turkey	0.53	1.08
Greece	0.12	0.33			
Luxembourg	0.12	0.12			
Cyprus	0.11	0.11			
Lithuania	0.11	0.11			
Latvia	0.10	0.10			
Slovenia	0.09	0.10			
Malta	0.08	0.09			
Estonia	0.07	0.08			
EU27	**28.54**	**26.32**	**Total non-EU**	**71.46**	**73.68**

Annex F. Constituencies on the Boards of the IMF and World Bank

Director (*alternate*)	EU	Other
Belgium (*Austria*)	**Austria, Belgium**, Czech Republic, Hungary, Luxembourg, **Slovak Republic, Slovenia**	Belarus, Kazakhstan, Turkey
Netherlands (*Ukraine*)	Bulgaria, **Cyprus, Netherlands**, Romania	Armenia, Bosnia and Herzegovina, Croatia, Macedonia, Moldova, Montenegro, Ukraine, Georgia, Israel
Spain (*Mexico*)	**Spain**	Costa Rica, El Salvador, Guatemala, Honduras, Mexico, Nicaragua, Venezuela, Bolivia
Italy (*Greece – IMF*) (*Portugal –WB*)	**Greece**, **Italy**, **Malta, Portugal**,	Albania, San Marino, Timor-Leste
Canada (*Ireland – IMF*) (*Barbados – WB*)	**Ireland**	Canada, Caribbean Islands
Denmark (*Norway*) – IMF Sweden (*Denmark*) – WB	Denmark, Estonia, **Finland**, Latvia, Lithuania, Sweden	Iceland, Norway
Switzerland (*Poland*)	Poland	Azerbaijan, Kyrgyz Republic, Serbia, Switzerland, Tajikistan, Turkmenistan, Uzbekistan

Notes: There are 6 permanent directors for France, Germany, UK, China, Russia and Saudi Arabia, without constituency attachments.

Eurozone states are in bold, and are present in 5 constituencies, in addition to the 2 permanent directors for France and Germany.

Two constituencies mix EU and non-European states – those led by Spain and Canada.

In addition there are 9 entirely non-European constituencies currently led by directors from Thailand, Korea, Egypt, Sierra Leone, Iran, Brazil, Argentina, India and Rwanda.

Annex G. Shareholdings in the EBRD (capital subscribed in € mil.)

EU		Non-EU	
France	1,704	United States	2,000
Germany	1,704	Japan	1,704
Italy	1,704	Russia	800
United Kingdom	1,704	Canada	680
Spain	680	Switzerland	456
Netherlands	496	Turkey	230
Austria	456	Australia	200
Belgium	456	Korea, Republic of	200
Sweden	456	Ukraine	160
Poland	256	Israel	130
Finland	250	Serbia	94
Norway	250	Croatia	73
Denmark	240	Kazakhstan	46
Czech Republic	171	Uzbekistan	42
Bulgaria	158	Belarus	40
Hungary	158	Bosnia and Herzegovina	34
Greece	130	Mexico	30
Romania	96	Albania	20
Slovak Republic	85	Azerbaijan	20
Portugal	84	Egypt	20
Ireland	60	Georgia	20
Slovenia	42	Iceland	20
Luxembourg	40	Kyrgyz Republic	20
Cyprus	20	Moldova	20
Estonia	20	Tajikistan	20
Latvia	20	FYR Macedonia	14
Lithuania	20	Armenia	10
Malta	2	Morocco	10
European Community	600	New Zealand	10
Euro. Investment Bank	600	Liechtenstein	4

		Montenegro	4
		Mongolia	2
		Turkmenistan	2
Total EU27	**12,660**	**Total non-EU**	**7,133**

Annex H. Constituencies on the Board of the EBRD

Director	EU	Other
Austria	Austria, Malta, Cyprus	Israel, Kazakhstan, Bosnia & Herzegovina
Italy	Italy	
Portugal, Greece	Portugal, Greece	
France	France	
Australia		Australia, Korea, New Zeeland, Egypt
Switzerland		Switzerland, Turkey, Liechtenstein, Uzbekistan, Kyrgyz Rep., Azerbaijan, Turkmenistan, Montenegro
EIB		
Sweden	Sweden, Estonia	Iceland,
Japan		Japan
United States		United States
Canada		Canada, Morocco
Denmark	Denmark, Ireland, Lithuania	Macedonia
Finland	Finland, Latvia	Norway
Russian Federation, Tajikistan, Belarus		Russian Federation, Tajikistan, Belarus
EU		
Spain	Spain	Mexico
Ukraine	Romania	Ukraine, Moldova, Georgia, Armenia
United Kingdom	United Kingdom	
Germany	Germany	
Belgium	Belgium, Luxembourg, Slovenia	
Bulgaria	Bulgaria, Poland	Albania
Czech Rep	Czech Rep, Hungary, Slovak Rep.	Croatia
Netherlands	Netherlands	Mongolia

Annex I. Extracts from the Lisbon Treaty

INTERNATIONAL AGREEMENTS

Article 216

1. The Union may conclude an agreement with one or more third countries or international organisations where the Treaties so provide or where the conclusion of an agreement is necessary in order to achieve, within the framework of the Union's policies, one of the objectives referred to in the Treaties, or is provided for in a legally binding Union act or is likely to affect common rules or alter their scope.

2. Agreements concluded by the Union are binding upon the institutions of the Union and on its member states.

Article 217 (ex Article 310 TEC)

The Union may conclude with one or more third countries or international organisations agreements establishing an association involving reciprocal rights and obligations, common action and special procedure.

Article 218 (ex Article 300 TEC)

1. Without prejudice to the specific provisions laid down in Article 207, agreements between the Union and third countries or international organisations shall be negotiated and concluded in accordance with the following procedure.

2. The Council shall authorise the opening of negotiations, adopt negotiating directives, authorise the signing of agreements and conclude them.

3. The Commission, or the High Representative of the Union for Foreign Affairs and Security Policy where the agreement envisaged relates exclusively or principally to the common foreign and security policy, shall submit recommendations to the Council, which shall adopt a decision authorising the opening of negotiations and, depending on the subject of the agreement envisaged, nominating the Union negotiator or the head of the Union's negotiating team.

4. The Council may address directives to the negotiator and designate a special committee in consultation with which the negotiations must be conducted.

5. The Council, on a proposal by the negotiator, shall adopt a decision authorising the signing of the agreement and, if necessary, its provisional application before entry into force.

6. The Council, on a proposal by the negotiator, shall adopt a decision concluding the agreement. Except where agreements relate exclusively to the common foreign and security policy, the Council shall adopt the decision concluding the agreement:

(a) after obtaining the consent of the European Parliament in the following cases:

(i) association agreements;

(ii) agreement on Union accession to the European Convention for the Protection of Human Rights and Fundamental Freedoms;

(iii) agreements establishing a specific institutional framework by organising cooperation

procedures;

(iv) agreements with important budgetary implications for the Union;

(v) agreements covering fields to which either the ordinary legislative procedure applies, or the special legislative procedure where consent by the European Parliament is required.

The European Parliament and the Council may, in an urgent situation, agree upon a time-limit for consent.

(b) after consulting the European Parliament in other cases. The European Parliament shall deliver its opinion within a time-limit which the Council may set depending on the urgency of the matter. In the absence of an opinion within that time-limit, the Council may act.

7. When concluding an agreement, the Council may, by way of derogation from paragraphs 5, 6 and 9, authorise the negotiator to approve on the Union's behalf modifications to the agreement where it provides for them to be adopted by a simplified procedure or by a body set up by the agreement. The Council may attach specific conditions to such authorisation.

8. The Council shall act by a qualified majority throughout the procedure.

However, it shall act unanimously when the agreement covers a field for which unanimity is required for the adoption of a Union act as well as for association agreements and the agreements referred to in Article 212 with the States which are candidates for accession. The Council shall also act unanimously for the agreement on accession of the Union to the European Convention for the Protection of Human Rights and Fundamental Freedoms; the decision concluding this agreement shall enter into force after it has been approved by the member states in accordance with their respective constitutional requirements.

9. The Council, on a proposal from the Commission or the High Representative of the Union for Foreign Affairs and Security Policy, shall adopt a decision suspending application of an agreement and establishing the positions to be adopted on the Union's behalf in a body set up by an agreement, when that body is called upon to adopt acts having legal effects, with the exception of acts supplementing or amending the institutional framework of the agreement.

10. The European Parliament shall be immediately and fully informed at all stages of the procedure.

11. A member state, the European Parliament, the Council or the Commission may obtain the opinion of the Court of Justice as to whether an agreement envisaged is compatible with the Treaties. Where the opinion of the Court is adverse, the agreement envisaged may not enter into force unless it is amended or the Treaties are revised.

Article 219 (ex Article 111(1) to (3) and (5) TEC)

1. By way of derogation from Article 218, the Council, either on a recommendation from the European Central Bank or on a recommendation from the Commission and after consulting the European Central Bank, in an endeavour to reach a consensus consistent with the objective of price stability, may conclude formal agreements on an exchange-rate system for the euro in relation to the currencies of third States. The Council shall act unanimously after consulting the European Parliament and in accordance with the procedure provided for in paragraph 3. The Council may, either on a recommendation from the European Central Bank or on a recommendation from the Commission, and after consulting the European Central Bank, in an endeavour to reach a consensus consistent with the objective of price stability, adopt, adjust or abandon the central rates of the euro within the exchange-rate system. The President of the Council shall inform the European Parliament of the adoption, adjustment or abandonment of the euro central rates.

2. In the absence of an exchange-rate system in relation to one or more currencies of third States as referred to in paragraph 1, the Council, either on a recommendation from the Commission and after consulting the European Central Bank or on a recommendation from the European Central Bank, may formulate general orientations for exchange-rate policy in relation to these currencies. These general orientations shall be without prejudice to the primary objective of the ESCB to maintain price stability.

3. By way of derogation from Article 218, where agreements concerning monetary or foreign exchange regime matters need to be negotiated by the Union with one or more third States or international organisations, the Council, on a recommendation from the Commission and after consulting the European Central Bank, shall decide the arrangements for the negotiation and for the conclusion of such agreements. These arrangements shall ensure that the Union expresses a single position. The Commission shall be fully associated with the negotiations.

4. Without prejudice to Union competence and Union agreements as regards economic and monetary union, member states may negotiate in international bodies and conclude international agreements.

Annex J. The Common Visa Application Centre in Moldova

The CVAC is located on the premises of the Hungarian Embassy in Chisinau.It is currently used by 12 EU states of the Schengen area: Austria, Belgium, Denmark, Estonia, Finland, Greece, Hungary, Latvia, Luxembourg, the Netherlands, Slovenia and Sweden.

The CVAC accepts applications for transit, airport transit and short-stay visas (A and C type Schengen visas) of up to 90 days for the participating countries. The Centre processes the visas for these countries in conformity with the general Schengen practice. The treatment and the decision on the application is taken by the member state responsible.

The applications are collected in the Centre (scanning of passports and pictures) and sent at least once a week to the processing consulates located elsewhere. Besides the hard copy of the application and the supporting documents, a reusable smart card with the basic data of the applicant and the application is attached to each application. The smart card contains the photo of the applicant and later the fingerprints as well.

The idea was born in order to avoid obliging all member states having to install the necessary equipment for enrolling biometric identifiers in every consular office. The CVAC at the Hungarian Consulate in Chisinau was set up following a Commission Proposal in May 2006 for a regulation on setting up a legal framework for the organisation of member states' consular offices to enhance consular cooperation. Moldova was identified as one of the most relevant countries for a pilot project as the accession of Romania created a new situation. Only a very small number of member states were represented in Chisinau and Romania had introduced the visa obligation for Moldovan citizens upon its EU accession. The Centre was officially opened on 25 April 2007, following the signature of a Hungary-Moldova memorandum of understanding and of bilateral agreements with the participating EU member states. It initially issued visas for six EU member states (Austria, Denmark, Estonia, Latvia, Slovenia and Hungary), and was later expanded to 12.

Sources: Andrei Avram and Dietmar Müller, "Moldova's border with Romania: challenges and perspectives after Romania's accession to the European Union", *South-East Europe Review*, 3/2008, pp. 399-429 and European Commission, "Opening of a 'Common Visa Application Centre' in Moldova", 25 April 2006 (http://www.cac.md).

Annex K. Statement by the E3+3 with the support of the EU High Representative following the adoption, 9 June 2010, of UN Security Council Resolution 1929 on the Iranian nuclear programme

The following statement was agreed by the Foreign Ministers of China, France, Germany, Russia, the United Kingdom and the United States, *with the support of the High Representative of the European Union:*

"We, the Foreign Ministers of China, France, Germany, Russia, the United Kingdom and the United States, would like to take this opportunity to reaffirm our determination and commitment to seek an early negotiated solution to the Iranian nuclear issue.

The adoption of UNSCR 1929, while reflecting the international community's concern about the Iranian nuclear programme and reconfirming the need for Iran to comply with the UN Security Council and IAEA Board of Governors requirements, keeps the door open for continued engagement between E3+3 and Iran.

The aim of our efforts is to achieve a comprehensive and long-term settlement which would restore international confidence in the peaceful nature of Iran's nuclear programme, while respecting Iran's legitimate rights to the peaceful use of atomic energy. We are resolute in continuing our work for this purpose. We also welcome and commend all diplomatic efforts in this regard, especially those recently made by Brazil and Turkey on the specific issue of the Tehran Research Reactor.

We reaffirm our June 2008 proposals, which remain valid, as confirmed by resolution 1929. We believe these proposals provide a sound basis for future negotiations. We are prepared to continue dialogue and interaction with Iran in the context of implementing the understandings reached during the Geneva meeting of 1 October 2009. *We have asked Baroness Ashton, the EU High Representative for Foreign Affairs and Security Policy, to pursue this with Dr. Saeed Jalili, Secretary of Iran's Supreme National Security Council at the earliest opportunity.*

We expect Iran to demonstrate a pragmatic attitude and to respond positively to our openness towards dialogue and negotiations."

[Emphasis added]

Annex L. Draft Resolution A/64/L67 of the UN General Assembly – Participation of the European Union in the work of the UN

The General Assembly,

Bearing in mind the role and authority of the General Assembly as a principal organ of the United Nations and the importance of its effectiveness and efficiency in fulfilling its functions under the UN Charter,

Recognising, further, that the current interdependent international environment requires the strengthening of the multilateral system in accordance with the purposes and principles of the United Nations and then principles of international law,

Acknowledging that, when an organisation for regional integration develops common external policies and establishes permanent structures for their conduct and representation, the General Assembly may benefit from the effective participation in its deliberations of that organisation's external representatives speaking on behalf of the organisation and its member states, without prejudice to the ability of each organisation to define the modalities of its external representation,

Recalling the long standing relations between the European Union and the United Nations,

Noting the entry into force on 1 December 2009 of the Treaty of Lisbon, through which the European Union has made changes to its institutional system, in particular as regards its external representation,

Noting that in the Treaty of Lisbon, the European Union reaffirms *inter alia* its commitment to the purposes and principles of the United Nations Charter and to the promotion of multilateral solutions to common problems, in particular in the framework of the United Nations,

Noting also that under the Treaty of Lisbon, the member states of the European Union have entrusted the external representation of the European Union, with regard to the exercise of the competences of the European Union provided for by the Treaty of Lisbon, to the following institutional representatives: the President of the European Council; the High Representative of the European Union for Foreign Affairs and Security Policy; and the European Commission and European Union Delegations,

Noting that the representatives of the European Union referred to above have assumed the role, previously performed by the representatives of the member state holding the rotating Presidency of the Council of the European Union, of acting on behalf of the European Union at the UN in the exercise of the competences conferred by its member states,

Recalling that, by virtue of the Lisbon Treaty, the European Union has replaced the European Community, as notified to the Secretary-General of the United nations by a letter dated 30 November 2009

Noting that the European Union is a party to many instruments concluded under the auspices of the United Nations, is a member of several United Nations specialised agencies and is a full participant in several United Nations bodies,

Noting that the European Union retains observer status in the General Assembly

1. *Decides* that the representatives of the European Union for the purpose of participating effectively in the sessions and work of the General Assembly, including in the general debate, and its committees and working groups, in international meetings and conferences convened under the auspices of the Assembly, as well as in United Nations conferences, and in order to present positions of the European Union, shall be invited to speak in a timely manner, similar to the established practice for representatives of major groups, without prejudice to the intergovernmental nature of the United Nations, shall be permitted to circulate documents, to make proposals and submit amendments, the right to raise points of order, but not to challenge decisions of the presiding officer, and to exercise the right of reply, and be afforded seating arrangements which are adequate for the exercise of the aforementioned actions; the European Union shall not have the right to vote or to put forward candidates in the General Assembly;

2. *Decides* that when a regional organisation representing member states has reached a level of integration that enables that organisation to speak with one voice, the General assembly my adopt modalities, in the spirit of this resolution, for the participation in its deliberations of that organisation's external representatives speaking on behalf of the organisation and its member states;

3. *Requests* the Secretary-General to take any measures necessary to ensure the implementation of this decision.

Note: this includes amendments to the prior text tabled by the European Union on 13 September 2010.

Annex M. UN General Assembly Voting on Motion to Adjourn the Debate on Participation of the EU in the UN, 13 September 2010

Regions	Yes			No	Abstain	
Africa	Algeria Angola Benin Botswana Burkina Faso Chad Comoros Congo Côte D'Ivoire Djibouti	Equatorial- Guinea Eritrea Ethiopia Ghana Kenya Lesotho Libya Mali Mauritania Mozambique	Namibia Nigeria Seychelles Somalia South Africa Sudan Togo Uganda Tanzania Zambia Zimbabwe	Liberia Malawi	Morocco Tunisia	Burundi Cameroon Central African- Republic Democratic- Republic of Congo	Gambia Rwanda Senegal
Americas	Antigua Barbuda Barbados Belize Bolivia Cuba Dominica Ecuador	El Salvador Grenada Guyana Haiti Jamaica Nicaragua St Knitts- Levis	St Lucia St Vincent- Gren Suriname Trinidad- Tobago Venezuela	Chile Colombia Costa Rica Guatemala Mexico	Panama Paraguay Peru United States Uruguay	Argentina Brazil Canada	Dominican-Rep. Honduras
Asia	China DPR Korea India Indonesia Malaysia	Philippines Singapore Thailand Turkmenistan		Afghanistan Bangladesh Cambodia Kazakhstan	Rep. of Korea Timór Leste Uzbekistan	Armenia Bhutan Brunei Mongolia	Nepal Pakistan Sri Lanka Darussalam

Europe	Russian Federation	Albania Andorra Austria Belgium Bosnia and Herzegovina Bulgaria Croatia Cyprus Czech Rep. Denmark Estonia Finland FYROM France Georgia	Germany Greece Hungary Iceland Ireland Italy Latvia Liechtenstein Lithuania Luxembourg Malta Monaco Montenegro Netherlands Norway Poland	Portugal Moldova Romania San Marino Serbia Czech Slovakia Slovenia Spain Sweden Switzerland Turkey Ukraine UK	Belarus
Middle East	Bahrain Iran Iraq Kuwait Lebanon	Qatar Saudi Arabia Syria Yemen	Israel	Jordan	Oman	UA Emirates
Oceania	Fiji Marshall Islands Micronesia	Nauru Palau Solomon Islands	Papua New Guinea Tonga	Tuvalu	Australia New Zealand	Samoa
Total	76		71			26

Annex N. Staffing in the Foreign Services of the EU and the MS[a]

	Number of missions [b]	Number of staff, [c] own nationals	Number of staff, locally employed	Total staff	Staff per capita (1 per head of capita)	Population millions
Germany	227	6,900	5,300	12,200	6,705	81.8
France	278	6,754	5,087	11,841	5,464	64.7
UK	226	4,863	8,792	13,655	4,540	62.0
Italy [d]	238	4,754	2,785	7,539	7,998	60.3
Spain	208	4,428	2,197	6,625	6,928	45.9
Belgium	128	1,943	1,418	3,361	3,213	10.8
Netherlands	137	3,016	1,512	4,528	3,666	16.6
Luxembourg	35	..	..	..	..	0.5
Austria	100	1,280	654	1,934	4,343	8.4
Denmark	119	1,450	1,233	2,683	2,050	5.5
Sweden	100	1,260	1,250	2,510	3,705	9.3
Finland	97	1,567	1,179	2,746	1,966	5.4
Ireland	75	1,100	300	1,400	3,214	4.5
Portugal	132	812	1,581	2,393	4,430	10.6
Greece	91	..	..	..	..	11.3
Malta	30	343	137	480	833	0.4
Cyprus	42	251	314	565	1,416	0.8
Poland	137	2,868	917	3,785	10,092	38.2
Czech Rep.	124	2,203	710	2,733	3,842	10.5
Slovakia	89	630	283	913	5,915	5.4
Hungary	102	1,766	673	2,439	4,100	10.0
Slovenia	46	641	260	901	2,220	2.0
Estonia	42	593	110	703	1,849	1.3
Latvia	55	513	79	592	3,716	2.2
Lithuania	59	554	270	824	4,005	3.3
Bulgaria	111	1,480	330	1,810	4,199	7.6
Romania	136	2,052	-	2,052	10,478	21.5
EU 27 total	3,164	55,441	38,471	93,912	5,335	501
EEAS	136	1.643	2.077	3,720	134,677	501
Commission						
Aidco	-	1,020	-	1,020		
ECHO	-	259	-	259		
Developmen	-	205	-	205		
Trade	-	574	-	574		
Total	-	3,701	-	5,778	86,708	501
US	265	21,872	6,010	27,882	11,125	310,2

[a] *Source:* Foreign ministry websites and correspondence with national mfa officials. ".." signifies that data have not been available to us, but the totals for EU27 include estimates for these countries.

[b] 'Missions' include embassies, missions, permanent representations, consulates and general consulates.

[c] 'Number of staff' only includes permanent, full-time employees.

[d] Includes staff at the Italian cultural institutes.

[e] This includes that part of DG Development that is not being moved into EEAS.

Annex O. Budget Expenditure on Diplomacy of the EU and Member States [a]

	Budget, millions	Budget per capita	Population, millions
Germany	€873	€10.67	81.8
France	€878	€13.57	64.7
UK	€635	€10.24	62.0
Italy [b]	€991	€16.43	60.3
Spain	€475	€10.35	45.9
Belgium	€211	€19.54	10.8
Netherlands	€502	€30.24	16.6
Luxembourg	..	..	0.5
Austria	€215	€25.60	8.4
Denmark	€253	€46.00	5.5
Sweden	€320	€34.41	9.3
Finland	€202	€37.41	5.4
Ireland	€168	€37.33	4.5
Portugal	€195	€18.40	10.6
Greece	..	..	11.3
Malta	€23	€57.50	0.4
Cyprus	€62	€77.50	0.8
Poland	€383	€10.03	38.2
Czech Rep.	€284	€27.05	10.5
Slovakia	€78	€14.44	5.4
Hungary	€91	€9.10	10.0
Slovenia	€73	€36.50	2.0
Estonia	€23	€17.70	1.3
Latvia	€35	€15.91	2.2
Lithuania	€48	€14.55	3.3
Bulgaria	€91	€11.97	7.6
Romania	€130	€6.05	21.5
EU 27 total [c]	**€7,529**	**€15.03**	**501**
EEAS	**€476**	**€0.95**	**501**
US	€8,359	€26.95	310.2

[a] *Source:* Foreign Ministry websites and correspondence with national officials. Expenditure for the most recent year on the administration of the foreign service at home in the capital and in embassies abroad. This includes all running expenditures (salaries, rent, office expenses, representational allowances, infrastructural expenses, telecoms, cultural programmes, etc); i.e. all expenditures, but **excluding** major operational programmes such as humanitarian and development aid, cultural programmes and trade promotion.
[b] Includes costs of the Italian cultural institutes.
[c] Total includes estimated data (indicated with) for several countries.

Annex P. Aid (ODA) Expenditures of the EU and Member States and Administering Departments

	Total gross ODA (€ millions)	Aid administration expenditure (€ millions) [a]	Executing department	Number of staff in executing department [b]
Germany	9,436	..	BMZ – Federal Ministry for Economic Cooperation and Development GTZ – Deutsche Gesellschaft für Technische Zusammenarbeit KfW – Kreditanstalt für Wiederaufbau	
France	9,790	66	Directorate General for Int'l Cooperation and Development, MFA (annual project expenditure)	1,236
		220	Agence Française de Développement	1,042
UK	9,061	199	DFID – Department for International Development	1,600
Italy	2,610	..	Italian Development Cooperation Programme, MFA	
Spain	5,175	..	Spanish Agency for Int'l Development Cooperation, MFA	1,246
Belgium	2,048	3,6	Federal Public Service of Foreign Affairs, Foreign Trade and Development Cooperation	65
Netherlands	5,060	231	Ministry of Development Cooperation, MFA	213
Luxembourg	317	8	Development Coop. and Humanitarian Affairs, MFA Lux-Development	109
Austria	902	12	Austrian Development Cooperation, MFA	..
Denmark	2,213	118	Danish International Development Agency, MFA	..
Sweden	3,580	100	Swedish Int'l Development Agency, MFA	773
Finland	1,012	13	Department for Int'l Development Cooperation, MFA	135

| 143

144 | ANNEXES

Ireland	787	32	Irish Aid, DFA	..
Portugal	399	7.6	Inst. Português de Apoio ao Desenvolvimento, MFA	154
Greece	478	..	Hellenic Aid, MFA	..
Malta	11	..	Overseas Development Policy, MFA	5
Cyprus	27	..	Cyprus Aid, MFA	5
Poland	270	..	Polish Aid, MFA	72
Czech Rep.	176	..	CZDA – Czech Development Agency, MFA	..
Slovakia	58	0.5	Slovak Aid, MFA	13
Hungary	91	0.3	Int'l Development Cooperation Department, MFA	12
Slovenia	52	..	Int'l Development Coop. and Humanitarian Assistance, MFA	..
Estonia	15	..	Estonian Development Cooperation, MFA	10
Latvia	16	..	Development Cooperation MFA	5
Lithuania	37	..	Development Coop. and Democracy Promotion Dept., MFA	18
Bulgaria	13	..	Development Cooperation, MFA	..
Romania	102	..	Development Assistance Division, MFA	7
EU27 total	53,736			
EC	12,092	221	AidCo, ECHO, Development DG [c]	1,484
EU grand total	65,776			
US	22,576		USAID – U.S. Agency for Int'l Development	

Sources: OECD/DAC for all OECD member states, http://www.oecd.org/dataoecd/17/9/4498l892.pdf; for non-OECD countries UN and Eurostat sources.

[a] Cost data in this column are not included in the figures in the preceding table on MFA costs.

[b] Number of staff does not include locally recruited employees.

[c] Including 2/3 of DG Development, the other 1/3 being transferred to EEAS.